NORWICH AT PEACE

This photograph of Norwich Market Place was taken just before the period covered by this book. A row of horse-drawn cabs waits on the Walk at the bottom of the market.

NORWICH AT PEACE

Joan Banger

POPPYLAND PUBLISHING

Picture credits

H. Frederick Low/Aerial Archaeology: front cover, page 81
Joan Banger collection: front cover, pages 2, 7, 9, 11, 16, 21, 24, 25, 36, 37, 39, 42, 43, 46, 52, 53, 55, 56, 61, 65, 66, 67, 68, 71, 74, 80, 83
G. A. F. Plunkett: pages 9, 14, 18, 19, 27, 31, 35, 45, 48, 60, 69, 75, 84
F. Neal: pages 6, 15, 23, 28, 50, 73
Christopher Pipe/Watermark: pages 26, 77, 78, 79
Poppyland Photos: pages 12, 20, 29, 32 (left), 33, 62
Keith Skipper: pages 54, 59
George Swain/Norfolk County Council Library & Information Service: pages 8, 13
Norfolk County Council Library & Information Service: pages 30, 32 (right), 38, 40, 44, 82

Support and resource information to accompany this book can be found by visiting <www.poppyland.co.uk> and clicking on the 'Support and Resources' button.

Dedication

Norwich is rich in having been the birthplace of many fine families – the Gurneys, Frys, Opies and Colmans, to name but a few: household names, not only in this city, but throughout the Kingdom.

I would like to dedicate this book to an unknown Norwich family, the Baileys. There are no monuments to their name, no church has a side chapel dedicated to their memory, but they were born, worked and lived in this city, and are part of its heritage; as are so many families although unrecorded by time.

A wedding in 1930s Norwich

Introduction

Norwich is a city situated near the East coast of England in the County of Norfolk. It is blessed by the miraculous survival of many architectural antiquities.

A Norman castle looks down on its bustling streets; its magnificent cathedral, founded in 1096, stands near the River Wensum which is crossed by many fine bridges and joins the River Yare so linking Norwich with the seaways of the world.

The origins of Norwich are obscure but historians believe it began as a group of Saxon settlements which in time merged to form a fortified town.

Its river links have helped to form its character. Many aliens have landed at its wharf to stay and merge their blood and cultures with those of its citizens.

Surrounded by a farming community, who share its shops and amenities, the small alleyways and narrow streets of Norwich contain a wealth of historical surprises: Elizabethan houses and delightful mediaeval, Tudor and Regency architecture link hands with sombre Victorian masonry under its multi-towered skyline which is now punctuated by immature buildings of concrete, steel and glass, standing embarrassed by the grandeur of their elder companions.

Throughout the years 1918 to 1939 strangers still settled within its long lost city gates, contributing to its changing pattern: planners designed, destroyed and rebuilt; businesses opened, flourished and died; births, marriages and deaths were registered; people laughed and cried.

In this book is recorded some of the domestic history of Norwich over that period – small incidents that did not shatter the world, but helped to shape the city.

Joan Banger's first title for Poppyland Publishing was *Norwich at War*, now in its third edition. It tells the story of Norwich in the period 1939–45, and is the standard account of Norwich through the years of the Second World War. Together with this title, you have a fascinating account of life in the city and its development over three decades.

As well as the books themselves, there are support materials on <www.poppyland.co.uk>, including an account from the author of how she began to write about the city's story. Click on the 'Support and Resources' button for these extra materials; use the catalogue pages to check availability of all our East Anglian titles.

The lumber market during the 1920s or early 1930s. All the buildings seen to the left of the Guildhall were shortly to be demolished to make way for the new City Hall.

Norwich Market Place in 1935: there is now a line of motor cars, but the old municipal offices have not yet been demolished.

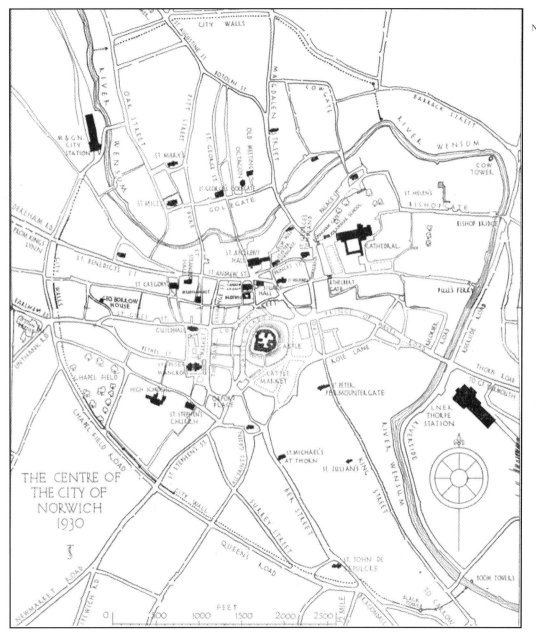

THE CENTRE OF
THE CITY OF
NORWICH
1930

1918

November

At 10.30 a.m. on Monday 11 November a message was received at the *Eastern Daily Press* office. It announced the longed-for ceasefire.

Europe had, for the previous four years, been engulfed in a World War. The people of Norwich had become so accustomed to its austerity that the end of the conflict seemed unbelievable.

Within moments of receiving the tidings, the newsmen displayed the magic words on flysheets outside their offices. In London Street, at the office of the Norfolk News Co. Ltd, the counters were besieged by people hungry to see the news in print.

The confirmation of the ceasefire spread like wildfire: people left their desks and workbenches, surging out into the streets; shopkeepers produced red, white and blue bunting and flags which were hung from all public buildings.

Peace was officially declared.

On the Saturday of Armistice weekend a new Lord Mayor was elected: Sir G. M. Chamberlin had the pleasure, at his first public speech, of expressing to King George V the joy of the people of Norwich at the cessation of hostilities. The new Lord Mayor's announcement was to have an immediate effect at the Guildhall. The

Celebrating the Armistice in Norwich Market Place

magistrates hearing evidence against the only two prisoners brought before them that day decided to dismiss the charges against them, on account of the wonderful news.

Outside the court, a holiday mood was developing. Hundreds of children, whose schools were closed because of an influenza epidemic, made their way to the Market Place where young people were marching, arms linked, along the Walk and London Street.

The numerous public houses that ringed the area were filled by merrymakers. Even the non-potent beverages that the war years had created sold out surprisingly quickly.

By early afternoon the crowds were increasing. They were entertained by a military parade. At three o'clock, five thousand troops, accompanied by their bands, marched into the Market Place. Brigadier General Shapley stood before the men as they formed ranks.

The Corporation joined the celebration; in full robes, and headed by the mace bearers, the Lord Mayor, Sheriff and Deputy Lord Mayor walked in solemn procession to stand under Lord Wellington's statue on the Market Place, the red and gold of their costumes supplying a splash of colour against the background of khaki uniforms.

The Lord Mayor called for three cheers; the crowds responded enthusiastically, while the soldiers removed their caps, placed them on their rifle ends, and held them aloft as they roared their delight.

The disbanding troops marched along the Walk back to their barracks, amid clapping and cheering crowds with arms outstretched towards them.

The increasing crowds stayed in the city centre throughout the afternoon. Street vendors appeared peddling victory motifs of red, white and blue, which were hurriedly purchased and pinned to hats and coat lapels.

The police relaxed and mingled with the crowds. There was a moment's fear when they saw their Chief Constable, Mr J. H. Dain, being surrounded by boisterous youngsters, but there was no cause for anxiety: the young people called for three cheers for the chief constable; his 150 policemen were popular and in no danger from the crowd.

As night fell, to the delight of all, street lights illuminated the city.

St Peter Mancroft church witnessed remarkable scenes as people started to queue an hour before the service of thanksgiving, which had been planned for eight o'clock. The vast crowd waited quietly for admis-

doctors were succumbing to infection, business houses were handicapped by absent workers, the very air of Norwich reeked of eucalyptus and camphor. The influenza which had broken out was not of the usual type; in some cases the symptoms were not unlike those of diphtheria and many Norwich people were dead or dying.

The Norfolk and Norwich Hospital prohibited visitors: it was thought that the overcrowded yards and alleys of Norwich were breeding grounds for the disease. Many of the houses were in a dilapidated condition and a single standpipe in an open drain often supplied many houses in cobbled yards, and their rows of outside privies contributed to the general lack of hygiene.

Family life was still disrupted. Many men were still serving in the Forces in Europe and thousands of prisoners of war were being discharged and were marching into France, hungry and dressed in rags. They were given neither food nor help on their pitiful 60-mile march to the French lines.

Norwich housewives were informed in November that they would soon be able to buy white bread again. The submarine menace was now over and there was a considerable amount of grain in the country. There was also to be offal available for pig feed.

St Peter Mancroft church and the Market Place, scene of many rejoicings

sion and somehow some two thousand people crowded into the church; they filled every available seat in the nave, choir and chapels, even sitting on the altar steps right up to the nave. The rigid class structure of the time was forgotten as gentry rubbed shoulders with workers.

Canon F. J. Meyrick conducted the service accompanied by a large number of clergy, including two army chaplains.

The service opened with the singing of the National Anthem, followed by the reading of Psalm 146 and then the clear voice of the new Lord Mayor reading the lesson.

Outside in the streets the usually sober-minded citizens abandoned all reserve. Although the authorities had prohibited the promiscuous discharging of fireworks, the police wisely turned a blind eye as youngsters threw fire crackers and coloured fire into the crowds.

The police had been worried that the celebrations might become completely out of hand but they could see that basically the joviality was under control.

Despite their joy, the people could not forget the problems of the baffling sickness that was sweeping the city: schools were already closed, proprietors of picture houses were excluding children under the age of 14,

This photograph of Old Brew Yard was taken in July 1937

December

The women whose husbands were desperately trying to get home to them looked forward to the first Christmas of peace.

Hopefully, they purchased small gifts: Black Prince tobacco at eight pence an ounce or gramophone records from Fieldings record shop in St Stephen's at one shilling and sixpence.

Officers' wives noted that Nickalls of Rampant Horse Street were selling 40-piece china tea services at 14 shillings and sixpence.

The women longed to show their menfolk the advert from the Norwich Corporation Electricity Department for the new form of illumination: this wonderful new invention could light a house for five farthings a day with neither smoke nor smell, and matches were never needed.

If they were planning a party for their returning men, the International Store had salmon at two shillings and three pence for a large tin. If the housekeeping money did not stretch to such luxury, there was the first National Kitchen which had been opened in November in Crooks Place. This, it had been stressed, was not a charitable institution in any sense of the word: rather, it was a local effort instigated by the government, to help the harassed housewife in her difficult task of providing a midday meal. It was an experimental project: if successful, more kitchens would be opened; if it made a loss, the entire scheme would be abandoned.

In the first week of December, General Election meetings were being held in Norwich. Polling day was 14 December. Norwich had three candidates: Lt Commander Hilton Young DSO, DSC was the dashing Liberal candidate, Mr G. H. Roberts the Coalition Labour candidate, and a very formidable figure, Mr H. E. Witard, once again fought the Labour cause.

At the beginning of the campaign Commander Young was still serving in North Russia. Until his return, his parents carried out his election meetings in Norwich.

Speaking at George White School on a Thursday night in December, Mr Witard reported that during the previous few days he had received threats to his life. However, he said, as he had been fighting the workers' cause for 25 years he was not likely to flinch at such threats.

As Christmas approached and the tiny jets of flame from the paraffin lamps on the Market Place stalls illuminated the fine array of plump chickens for sale, it did not seem to matter that geese and foods were in short supply: a festive atmosphere prevailed.

On Christmas Eve a glittering hoar frost covered the rooftops and canvas of the stalls. It gave the appearance of a tranquil, white Christmas. Norwich, and the World, was at peace!

1919

January

As the men who had already returned settled down into civilian life in the New Year, they found the weather kind; light southerly winds blew as they took their families to see *Mother Hubbard*, the pantomime showing at the Hippodrome, St Giles.

The Electric Cinema in Prince of Wales Road was showing the enormously successful six-part production of *The Correspondent* and on the same programme Pearl White and Antonio Morenoir starred in the seat-hugging serial *The House of Fate*. The charming songstress, Alice Fairland, completed the programme.

Men returning to their girlfriends could find diamond rings, containing five diamond settings, for twenty five shillings at H. Samuels in the Walk.

Houses were available to rent at five shillings and sixpence to seven shillings a week. Many couples looked longingly at the houses on Unthank Road being sold for £550 but, for many, this was far beyond their means, as were the OK Junior four-stroke motor cycles being sold at Rudge-Whitworth Ltd in Prince of Wales Road which cost forty-four pounds, two shillings – even though they were advertised as being 5% below their pre-war price.

Food rationing continued, and it was thought that, in that form, it would cease at the beginning of May. However, it was believed rationing would still continue but in a less restrictive form.

The hope of returning to a Utopia fit for heroes was soon shattered as men searched for jobs but found none available.

The City became a place of unrest: pent up emotions exploded in the last week of the Old Year when a constable arrested a soldier at the Fun Fair at the Agricultural Hall. The policeman was somewhat rough in his handling of the soldier, excitement broke out, a yelling mob followed the officer and his

Prince of Wales Road was one of Norwich's 'new' roads, created to link the city centre with Norwich Thorpe railway station.

prisoner up London Street and, when the man was taken to the Guildhall, the crowd stoned the building, breaking several windows including those of the Chief Constable's office! The crowd surged around Market Place, in an ugly mood, for over an hour.

Later that week a further outbreak of hooliganism was witnessed around the Agricultural Hall. On this occasion, though, greater tact was shown by the police and the crowd was held under control.

The Agricultural Hall (which in 1959 became the home of Anglia Television) was very popular with the people of Norwich. The red stone and brick building opposite the Royal Hotel in Prince of Wales Road had been opened by the Prince of Wales in 1882. The main hall was one hundred and forty-seven feet long and ninety-eight feet wide and included removable wrought iron pens for cattle shows. The building also contained a kitchen and dining room and, on the ground floor, a buffet, ladies' room, board room and offices.

On three sides of the hall were galleries with cranes for raising exhibitions. Over the main entrance and offices was a large room containing a stage ninety-seven feet long by forty-eight feet wide which was available for public assemblies. There was also an assembly room with seating for 850 people and the building was licensed for theatrical and other entertainments.

Because of their rowdy behaviour in and around the building, it was put out of bounds to soldiers, who risked not only the wrath of the local constabulary but also that of the military police. This unrest was to continue over many weeks.

Norwich Corporation was aware of the need to replace the slums with decent housing. It had been looking for some time for a suitable site, and now agreed to purchase Harford Hall Estate, containing around 150 acres, for the sum of £13,100. It was hoped that the land could be used for council housing and other schemes they had in mind.

The Corporation had also been considering ideas for a suitable War Memorial, and a very interesting suggestion had been made by the Lord Mayor: he wanted to see the establishment of a University College in Norwich. There was a magnificent response to his proposal, with promises of donations totalling £35,000 being made in the space of a few days. Another suggestion put forward was the erection of a new City Hall. This was at a time when the City Council was being asked to put forward schemes of work for the hundreds of unemployed men in the City.

During January, an acute concern for the Council was that, because the broads and rivers around Norwich had been flooded for nearly a month, the rat population was moving from the marshland into the surrounding built-up areas. Winter-stored root crops were being systematically raided and householders were even losing tablets of soap, the rats carrying them away as if there was no other source of food. One family reported the loss of a pet dove: its cage had been broken into and the dove eaten.

The rural authorities tried to control the problem and spent hundreds of pounds in the attempt. A bounty was paid for rats' tails but it was found that people living in a district where the bounty was a penny a tail were taking their tails to another district where they were paid twopence a tail. It was even hinted that some Norfolk boys were breeding litters of young rats for slaughter, to provide a continuing source of income.

February

During February, permission was sought to borrow several thousand pounds to extend and improve the City's electricity system.

It was announced during the month that three Norwich policewomen who carried out the work of matron, female searcher etc. were to be paid a clothing allowance. Mrs Trim and Mrs Hindes were to be paid three shillings a week, while Mrs Clark's allowance was four shillings.

At this time, police constables were paid seventy shillings a week on appointment, rising to ninety-five shillings after 22 years' service.

March

At a meeting of the Health Insurance Committee, attention was called to the rapid increase in tuberculosis cases in Norwich. Efforts to check the disease had so far proved unsuccessful. Large numbers of men discharged from the Army had been tubercular. It was agreed that arrangements for the use of the pavilion in the grounds of the isolation hospital should be extended. However, apart from tuberculosis, general health was surprisingly good.

April

Mr G. H. Roberts, speaking at the Savage Club, reported that sections of the population were talking openly of revolution because of the hundreds of Norwich workmen who were unemployed.

May

There was a new pay settlement by the boot and shoe manufacturers, which in general terms provided for a minimum wage of fifty-six shillings a week to be paid to men over 23 years of age, in return for a 48-hour week. Most Norwich shoe factories agreed to accept this policy.

At this time, unemployment pay for a man with a family of four children was fifty shillings a week. Unrest was rife. Twelve hundred clothing workers went on strike from Messrs James Southill and Company and 300 men at the Gas Company stopped work, although thankfully this stoppage lasted only for a few hours.

There was a very sad occasion this month: at around 5 o'clock a special train arrived at Thorpe Station, to be met by an escort of the Norfolk Regiment. It carried the body of Nurse Edith Cavell. She had been born at Swardeston on 4 December 1865. She had worked as matron of the Berkendael Medical Institute in Brussels, which had later become a military hospital renowned for hiding wounded English and French soldiers.

She had been shot on 12 October 1915, and her body was being brought to rest in her native county.

Her coffin was placed on a gun carriage drawn by four horses and crowds lined the streets as the solemn procession passed by. She was laid to rest in the quiet patch of green known as Life's Green, at the rear of Norwich Cathedral.

June

The Royal Norfolk Agricultural Show opened at its old venue, Eaton Park. It was a brilliant success: the weather was blazing hot and nearly 37,000 people attended – twice the attendance of the last show, held in 1914.

Traffic was becoming a problem in Norwich. Motorised vehicles did not mix readily with plodding hackney carriages and horse-drawn drays. In June, two cyclists were killed through collisions with motor cars, and an old lady was killed when a runaway horse smashed into a dairy in the too-aptly named Rampant Horse Street.

July

A beautiful day dawned on 19 July for the peace celebrations. A service was held at the Cathedral and the nave was a vast living mosaic of colour as the 4th Dragoon Guards, with the gay yellow facings of their uniforms

and their breasts covered by ribbons, were joined by men of the Royal Air Force, Royal Engineers, Royal Norfolks, Rifle Corps, Special Constables, the Boy Scouts and girls of the Land Army. Standing out, like small islands, were men of the Royal Navy and boys of the training brig *Nelson*.

As the great mosaic passed out of the cathedral, the 7th Dragoons led the procession to the Market Place. Behind them came Mounted Police, the Band of the Dragoons, 50 NCOs of the Royal Norfolks and 100 men of the Royal Air Force. They, in turn, were followed by 100 women of the Red Cross, nurses, firemen, school cadets and members of the private city fire brigades, the brigades of Messrs J. J. Colman, Caley and Sons and Boulton and Paul. All marched towards the Market Place, filling the area with a magnificent blaze of colour.

The Chief Constable, Mr Dain, later congratulated the organisers on the fact that the proceedings had passed off without a hitch.

A strange shadow passed over the city on 12 July when the airship R33 sailed over. Small children gasped in amazement and all heads turned up to the sky in astonishment.

During this month it was decided that, due to the alarming deterioration in coal stocks, deliveries were not to exceed two hundredweight to any one householder in any week. This was a worrying development, since most households used coal as fuel for cooking.

The Watch Committee was becoming very concerned about the morality of some films. They upheld the action of the Chief Constable who had forbidden the screening of a film called *The Girl Who Did Not Know*. He believed it was concerned primarily with seduction of women: one young woman was seduced then deserted by her lover, and committed suicide; another young woman was seduced by the proprietor of a gaming house and acted as his decoy, before also attempting to commit suicide. The proprietor was burnt to death in a motor car accident.

However, there was some opposition to local censorship. It was thought to be unsatisfactory that a film forbidden to be screened in Norwich was shown in other towns and cities without objection. Films were not the only type of entertainment subject to censorship: the variety show at the Electric Theatre had been subject to objections by the Chief Constable because immoral suggestions were used in one variety act.

Objections were made to another film, *Where Are My Children*,

Edith Cavell's funeral cortège in Norwich Cathedral Close

The old police office in the Market Place (photograph taken in September 1936). Clearly they needed a new building!

because it dealt with the subject of abortion and in one scene a woman was shown attending a doctor's surgery for that purpose.

September

The police remained preoccupied by the need to protect the people of Norwich from such vice and corruption.

At this time, the police were thought to be run effectively. New rates of pay had been announced from the beginning of the month and the rates for Police Constables were to range between £3 10s and £4 15s a week.

During the month, a total of 57 prisoners were conveyed to Norwich Prison – a decrease of nine on the same month in 1918.

During the year, the police granted licenses in the City as follows :

Pedlars	85
Hackney Carriages	69
Hackney Carriage Drivers	103
Tram Cars	42
Tram Car Drivers	65
Tram Car Conductors	148
Motor Buses	20
Motor Bus Drivers	34
Motor Bus Conductors	27
Explosives (Fireworks & Gunpowder)	71
Petroleum	70
Carbide of Calcium	34
Game Dealers	16
Street Traders (Children) – Year to September	108

November

Lakenham School, which was built in 1914 at a cost of £12,000, had been taken over by the War Office throughout the war and used as a military hospital. In November it reopened as a school.

The Norwich Players were performing four plays at the Old Music House, King Street, this month, presented by Nugent Monck. He had founded the Guild of Norwich Players in 1911, and Norwich theatre-going audiences were delighted with the performances. The Old Music House had been retained for Mr Monck rent-free throughout the war years.

December

As Christmas 1919 approached, money seemed to be more plentiful. The shops were filled with displays of goods. Messrs Garland, in London Street, was well-stocked in each of its 25 departments. Any mistress in search of useful presents for her domestic staff could choose from a satisfying variety of maids' dresses and caps.

Messrs Greens of The Walk were a little concerned that the dancing boom was putting considerable pressure on their stock of dress suits, dress shirts and the like. Curl's in Rampant Horse Street had dainty blouses in crêpe de chine and Japanese silk for 18s 11d, while Chamberlin's in Guildhall Hill was well stocked with good old fashioned Yuletide presents. The year was rapidly coming to a close.

1920

The many and conflicting rumours of rate increases abated when the weather became fine and sunny for the remaining days of the four-day holiday period.

The first week in January was chosen for the second National Rat Killing Week. Bubonic plague had struck again in Europe. In Norwich, everyone was saying that every week should be a rat-killing week and the city was divided into eight sections, with each one being allocated a man experienced in handling ferrets. The factories were using poison: in three months 1,500 visits were made by rat catchers to homes, shops and factories. Nearly 4,000 rats were killed by ferrets and it was impossible to number those killed by poison. During the first week of the campaign, some of the rat catchers' victims were

*The Walk, as
it was in 1915.
Note the soldiers
in uniform, the
open-topped tram
and the prevalence
of horse and cart
as a means of
transport.*

Cattle and sheep were sold at the market in the Castle Meadow throughout the period covered by this book.

laid out at Market Hall, and one rat measured 19 inches from head to tail.

During January the unemployment figures for December 1919 were published and showed that 2,585 Norwich men were unemployed, 2,043 of them ex-Service men.

The harshness of the times was reflected in the sentence passed on an 11-year-old Aylsham lad, convicted by the Juvenile Court of stealing one pound fifteen shillings. The Justices ordered that he be given six strokes of the birch rod and placed under the supervision of the probation officer for 12 months; his parents were ordered to restore the amount stolen and pay costs of fifteen shillings.

April

Norfolk Education Committee discussed increasing teachers' salaries and recommended that the annual pay of head masters should increase from £400 to £500 a year. One head master not affected by this change was Mr

Walter Scott, Head Master of Norwich School of Art: he was retiring after thirty years of service at the school.

Messrs Thurston opened their annual Tombland Fair. This year there was a new attraction: a super new roundabout, built at a cost of £22,000, called the Golden Dragon.

May

Norwich Council decided to proceed with the erection of 1,200 houses in the Angel Road area, but there was a snag: the work could only be done when funds were available.

It was during this month that the full extent of the social unrest in Norwich was realised. There was dissatisfaction with working conditions and disappointment with high prices; the reconstruction was too slow and the homes promised for returning soldiers had not materialised. The war had involved a huge national effort and, now that it was over, the nation's hopes and dreams were not being realised: the let-down was immense.

One of the major worries was increasing food prices: flour this month had jumped in price to nineteen shillings and threepence a sack.

At least the weather was good, which helped. Another bright spot was that the City Council had agreed contracts for building 100 concrete and steel houses. However, it was a sobering thought that, at this rate of progress, it would take a generation to make up housing needs. There was a feeling that the birth rate had dropped because the potential parents did not have homes.

June

By this month, Norwich District Committee's funds were exhausted and working people were being pressed to the utmost by inflated prices. The costs of labour and materials were rising to tremendous heights and rates were increasing.

A further body blow was dealt to the County when an outbreak of foot and mouth disease was reported on Norfolk farms. At Martham, 43 cattle and 182 sheep had to be slaughtered at just one farm.

At an auction at the Royal Hotel, the following properties were for sale:

56 Cecil Road	*let at £16 p.a., withdrawn at £225*	
58 Cecil Road	*let at £16 p.a., withdrawn at £222 10s 0d*	
(These were both leasehold for 75 years from October 1989)		
27 Rowington Road		
	let at £21 p.a. leasehold from February 1903, sold for £280	
68 Christchurch Road	*let at £26 p.a., sold for £520*	
1 Colman Road	*let at £32 10s 0d p.a., sold for £450*	
82 Mornington Road	*let at £19 p.a., sold for £450*	
18 & 19 Press Lane, Aylsham Road	*withdrawn at £115*	
14 Parker Road	*withdrawn at £320*	
21 St Stephens Square	*sold for £200*	
23 St Stephens Square	*sold for £200*	
17 Timberhill *freehold shop and dwelling house*	*sold for £150*	
53 Leicester Street	*let at £15 3s 4d p.a., sold for £137 10s 0d*	

July

Life still carried on as normal for some. The Norwich Regatta and Aquatic Festival revived its post-war festival in July. Mr Russell J. Colman kindly placed his Whitlingham grounds at the disposal of the promoters.

Norwich workers, meanwhile, were wondering whether they could afford to pay £1 a week for the newly built council houses and many Councillors felt that 12 shillings was the maximum they should be asked to pay.

August

The Unemployment Benefit Act 1920 received the Royal Assent in August. It provided for contributions to be:

men aged 18 and over:	employer 4*d*	employee 4*d*
women aged 18 and over:	employer 3½*d*	employee 3*d*
boys aged 16–18:	employer 2*d*	employee 2*d*
girls aged 16–18:	employer 2*d*	employee 1½*d*

Unemployment benefit was to be 15 shillings a week for men and 12 shillings for women. Those aged 18 and under were entitled to half the adult rate. No benefit was payable for the first three days of unemployment.

September

The tension continued to increase and in September there were remarkable scenes in the Council Chamber when mass demonstrations of unemployed men called attention to their grave plight. There were 5,000 men out of work in the city.

The Council was shaken and disappointed that the scheme to fund a University College as a war memorial had to be abandoned, because of shortage of funds. The project would have taken £100,000: the £60,000 raised became something of an embarrassment. A meeting was called to decide whether the people who had made donations should have them returned or should be asked for alternative suggestions.

October

The press reported plans for the construction of a super cinema in Prince of Wales Road, on the site of the Alexandra Mansions. Costing £70,000 to build, it would have seating for 2,000 people.

Cinematography had made enormous strides since the Theatre de Luxe in St Andrews made its appearance in April 1910. Since that time, a number of new cinemas had been established, but the old Theatre de Luxe had continued to hold its own against the newer competition.

The Theatre de Luxe, St Andrews

November

The newspapers began to speak of the closure of boot and shoe factories – one of the main industries in the city – and this highlighted the sense of hopelessness of the economic situation.

The government had realised the previous month that the magnitude of the crisis was such that special measures must be taken. The regular police forces and the small force of Special Constables were insufficient to control the civil unrest, they believed, and so they invited Lord Mayors throughout the land to take steps to form a Citizens' Guard to assist the police in safeguarding the nation.

Startling statements were made at a meeting of the Norwich Distress Committee. Some citizens, it was said, were on the verge of starvation and were having to pawn their worldly possessions to buy bread.

Thousands of people in Norwich were unemployed, and unless some direct action was taken to alleviate the distress men would become so desperate that the city would be plagued by thieving.

In spite of the general distress and unrest, the 41st Fat Stock Show opened at the Agricultural Hall. Cattle entries numbered 62 and there were 15 sheep pens and 17 pig pens on display in the main hall. A large number of manufacturers exhibited machinery and other agricultural items.

Norwich's small private schools continued to flourish: Pembroke House School on Unthank Road advertised kindergarten classes (morning only) at one guinea a term; junior classes at two guineas, upper classes three guineas and Swedish drill, an extra, was on offer for 10s 6d a term. Elocution lessons were available for a further guinea.

December

The unemployed were becoming desperate. On 22 December, a large crowd of them gathered near the Guildhall and at 5 o'clock they moved down London Street, halting in front of the International Stores. Somebody threw a stone through the window of the store and the crowd swept into the shop, breaking more windows as they surged forward. Cakes, fruit and bacon were looted as the crowd rampaged past the counters; people in the shop were alarmed; women screamed and cried.

The police moved in quickly and the situation, which had seemed totally out of control, was quickly stabilised.

As Christmas approached, the unbelievable happened: people calling at

Farrows Bank on the Walk, hoping to withdraw money to buy Christmas presents, found a small, grim-faced crowd at the door staring at a notice pinned to the door: 'Payments Suspended'. The bank was closed; its directors had been arrested. Mr Thomas Farrow, the Chairman, Mr Walter Crotch, a director, and Mr F. D. T. Hart were later charged with publishing a false annual report. Many families were to lose all their savings. It was a black Christmas for many Norwich people.

A noticeable feature of Christmas 1920 was the great reduction in the number of letters and Christmas cards posted. It was thought this was a direct result of the increase both in the number of people out of work and in postage prices.

1921

The past year's disarray continued into 1921. In January, a mass meeting of unemployed Norwich people was held at the Drill Hall, Chapelfield, to demand schemes of adequate maintenance, until such time as suitable schemes of work were available. Their spokesman, Mr Witard, asked whether there was any truth in the rumours circulating round the city that

the amount of relief paid was to be reduced. The previous week, it had been 12 shillings for married adults, 8 shillings for single people living at home, 12 shillings for single people in lodgings and 8 shillings for children.

A Norwich Council spokesman confirmed that the married person's relief was to be reduced from 12 to 9 shillings a week.

Mr Farrow and his colleagues from the ill-fated Farrows Bank failed to produce the necessary bail. The Chairman of the bank, Mr Thomas Farrow, was under the care of the prison doctor at Brixton Prison, too ill to be moved.

A bombshell was dropped on rate payers in January, causing something close to panic: it was decided to raise the poor rate from three shillings and sixpence to six shillings and ten pence in the pound for the half year. The rate was announced at 32 shillings and two pence in the pound to help provide unemployment relief. Some people were saying openly that it would prove impossible to collect so high a rate. Norwich was thought to be one of the most expensively rated boroughs in England.

The Chief Constable expressed his belief that unless the order for the increase was revoked, riots would be organised in the city and damage to property, and possibly even to life, could ensue.

Also this month, Norwich Corporation declared that water was to cost more. The Corporation had purchased the water works, and the citizens of Norwich were saying 'I told you so', while the Corporation insisted that the increase was attributable entirely to higher working costs, and could in no way be blamed on the transfer of ownership.

With money so short, the city's shops were all holding sales: Messrs Green, The Walk, were holding a 'Slump Sale'. Smart tweed overcoats for boys and girls were advertised for 18 and 11 shillings; a number of ladies' skirts were the same, while stylish men's overcoats, well cut from Navy Melton Blanket Cloth, were reduced from £5 to 35s 6d.

February

His Majesty King George V and Queen Mary, accompanied by Princess Mary, paid a surprise informal visit to Norwich in February, to inspect work being undertaken on unemployment relief housing schemes.

On Mile Cross Estate there were many Council houses in various

The Drill Hall tower, Chapelfield

Shops on the Mile Cross Estate, photographed in 2003

stages of construction, and the royal party were conducted round a group of houses at an advanced stage of erection. An explanation of the scheme and the method of construction was given to them. About 100 acres in extent, the Mile Cross Estate was a scene of great activity: in addition to the 100 houses being built, roads and sewage schemes were well under way. In all, 100 previously unemployed men were hard at work.

His Majesty commented to the Chairman of the Unemployed Workmen's Committee: 'I am sure we are doing everything we possibly can to help you, we sympathise very much with you in the trouble you are in, and hope it is not going to last very long.'

Unemployed people continued to make their dissatisfaction evident. In February they demanded that the Norwich Board of Guardians put schemes of work into action and the maximum out relief be increased from 27s 6d to £3 4s a week.

Twelve hundred unemployed Norwich men marched to the Guardians' Office and workhouse. Ugly scenes developed and a police constable was injured. Three arrests were made.

The proceedings began shortly after 2 p.m., when over a thousand unemployed men gathered on the market place. After speeches had been made the procession moved on, headed by a red flag on which was inscribed: 'Norwich Unemployed Men and Women: We demand work not dole'.

A further blow was dealt to the unemployed and other people on low incomes when the Norwich Gas Company announced it was seeking increases of 80%.

Matters began to come to a head when the Rate Payers Association and the local branch of the Middle Classes Union combined against the unemployed rate and refused to pay their taxes. The situation threatened to become disastrous, taking Norwich to the brink of bankruptcy.

The leaders of the Rate Payers Association and the Middle Classes Union were threatened with legal action: the Council said it had the power to collect rents from the tenants of landlords until such time as they paid the rates.

April

In April, Norwich honoured one of its illustrious sons, John Crome, who had died 100 years previously leaving behind him a wealth of paintings of Norwich and Norfolk. The City decided that everything in its power should be done to honour his name, and a memorial exhibition was mounted at the Castle Museum. His Majesty the Prince of Wales was asked to perform the opening ceremony.

May

There was more trouble from the local gasworks during this month as the workers went out on strike, refusing to unload French coal at Norwich wharf.

On the last Saturday in May, the Pavilion of the Eaton Golf Club, Newmarket Road, was destroyed by fire.

June

June saw the end of the 13-day trial of the directors of Farrows Bank. They were found guilty, and the sentences imposed by the court were:

Thomas Farrow, aged 58: 4 years' penal servitude.
William Walter Crotch, aged 48: 4 years' penal servitude.
F. D. Tabrum Hart, Auditor, aged 44: 12 months' imprisonment.

August

A new pavilion for Eaton Golf Club had been built on the site of the one destroyed by fire and on a Thursday afternoon in August the Lord Mayor, Col. Granville Duff M C, opened the new building.

November

At the Norwich municipal elections there were four Labour gains, and the composition of the new Council was:

> Liberal: 23
> Conservative: 21
> Labour: 15
> Independent: 2
> Rate Payers: 2
> Federation: 1

On 12 November one of the most violent storms in living memory swept over East Anglia. On that Sunday morning a 100 miles an hour hurricane swept through the city; practically every main road leading out of the city was blocked by falling trees, tiles, slates and chimney pots.

December

At 2.30 p.m. on 12 December the Picture House, Haymarket, reopened after extensive refurbishment. Admission prices were 10 shillings to boxes seating four people, and 2*s*, 1*s* 6*d* and 1*s* for seats in the Grand Circle and Stalls. A factory adjacent to the original cinema had been demolished to enlarge the building and it was renamed the Haymarket Picture House.

By December, local shops were experiencing a small boom in trade, but an increase in spending power was not experienced by the area's farm workers. They were faced with a reduction in their wage to 30 shillings a week. When they complained that this was not a living wage, the farmers told them they were 40% better off than they had been before the war and that, in their opinion, 30 shillings a week was a fair wage for the time.

A week before Christmas, two 12-year-old schoolboys marred their good

Bull Close School

records when they raided their Bull Close school. They stole £3 worth of sweets, toys, crackers and mince pies from Christmas trees which stood in classrooms.

This small criminal act seemed to reflect the desperation and poverty of so many working families. The boys were sentenced to 12 months' probation, which in 1921 amounted to a lenient punishment.

1922

The New Year was heralded by violent thunderstorms, which caused the River Yare to burst its banks in many places.

The coastline of East Anglia suffered when the low-lying areas of Yarmouth were flooded; parts of Lowestoft, in the vicinity of the Bridge and North Plain, also suffered, as did the North Denes.

The sea water overflowed the quay walls at Wells. Considerable damage was inflicted on Mundesley and there was great anxiety at Blakeney where the bank protecting the grazing marshes was severely tested. Fortunately, the bank withstood the strains.

The River Yare offered some hope to the unemployed during the month, when an extensive scheme of river widening was unveiled. Norwich City Council also agreed to a scheme to remove the existing granite setts in King Street, replacing them in part of the street with asphalt.

The Norwich Electric Tramways Company agreed to contribute £3,000 towards the cost of this work.

There was yet another industrial crisis in January, when the Boot and Shoe Operative Union rejected the new wage settlements which reduced its members' pay by four shillings a week for men and two shillings a week for women, with proportionate decreases in piece-work rates.

The newly rebuilt and enlarged Haymarket Picture House was showing The Fifth Form at St Dominic's. Additional attractions on the programme were: The Challenge of the Law, a thrilling story of Canadian life; and a third film called The Misfit's Wife. The night's entertainment was completed by a variety act starring George Bolton in songs and skits by the piano.
    Later in the month leading musicians from the Norwich Orchestras of the Norwich Hippodrome, Theatre Royal, Theatre de Luxe and Electric Theatre visited H. M. Prison at Mousehold to give a concert.

March

The Chief Constable, Mr Dain, gave a talk on crime in the city. He reported that the current strength of the Norwich Police Force was 146, together with 14 men enrolled as First Constables, who were held for reserve duty in the event of an emergency. The Reserve Special Constables comprised 207 citizens who were equipped with uniforms but who had agreed to serve without pay if they were needed in an emergency.

July

The *Norwich Mercury* printed details of a wonderful free offer to its readers: it offered free insurance against all fatal accidents to those readers who registered at newsagents for a regular supply of newspapers. The insurance would pay £20 plus £1 a week for 10 weeks to members of the deceased person's family in the event of accidental death.

On 29 July, the Mercury apologised to its readers for appearing in a somewhat unusual format: provincial printing trade union members had come out on strike, and so the usual 12-16 page paper was reduced to eight pages. Even so, there was still room for Messrs Dunlop to advertise their range of tyres.

Bicycle tyres ranged in price from 11s 6d to 18s 6d.
    With the ever increasing number of motor cars on the streets of Norwich, the Tyre Services Depot of 4 Castle Meadow advertised the fact that they could save motorists money: 28 x 3 tyres cost 47s 6d and the large 920 x 120 tyres cost 90s 5d.

September

On the twelfth of this month, all roads into Norwich seemed to lead to the Nest football ground where the Norwich Canaries were to replay their English Cup game with Barnsley. Railway excursion trains were running from all parts of East Anglia and some 12,000 spectators were there to roar their delight when Norwich scored the first goal. However, Barnsley scored two goals and victory slipped from the Canaries' grasp: they were out of the Cup.

October

The City Council approved extensive schemes of unemployment relief, to be put into operation over the winter months. The total cost of the works approved was expected ultimately to exceed £50,000, increasing the City's commitments to around half a million pounds. The nagging thought in many minds was that unemployment was not a temporary problem which would just go away.

November

The General Election was held in November. In Norwich, there were no Conservative candidates. The Liberals gave their support to Lieutenant Commander Hilton Young, a sitting member, and the other sitting member was Mr S. G. H. Roberts, an Independent. The Labour candidates were Messrs Witard and Johnson.

    Polling day, 8 November, was quiet and there was little noticeable enthusiasm until the evening. Few posters were to be seen and Labour sympathisers had chalked their slogans on the pavements.
    At 10.00 p.m. the *Mercury* screen, perched high above the tea room of Messrs Jarrold and Sons, started to flash the election results. By eleven o'clock there were many thousands of people gathered in the Market

Place. They were still there after midnight, shouting and singing. The final results for the two Norwich seats were:

G. H. Roberts (Ind)	31,167
Cmdr E. Hilton Young (Lib)	31,151
H. E. Witard (Lab)	15,609
G. F. Johnson (Lab)	14,490

On Thursday 9 November, a new Lord Mayor was elected. He was Mr George Henry Morse, leader of the local Conservative Party and a former Mayor.

December

As the excitement of the General Election died down, and Christmas approached, it was hoped that, this year, Christmas would mark a turning point which would result in an increase in world trade and a return to full employment.

The shops were well stocked over the Christmas period, and many shops had made sweeping reductions in their prices – a great boon to poorer households.

Just how hard pressed many were was reflected in the fact that, on one day in the Christmas week, 174 people were summonsed for non-payment

of rates. On the following day, a further 30 people were summonsed.

Lipton's, the well known chain store, announced it would distribute 10,000 Christmas parcels of groceries and many Norwich families benefited from this gesture.

The Doll's House, 20 Royal Arcade, dressed its windows with boxes of Arctic Frosted Christmas decorations, priced at sixpence a box.

The Post Office established a new record when it delivered 2,000,000 letters and newspapers and 150,000 parcels.

The year ended as it had begun: Christmas Day 1922 established another record as being one of the wildest since weather records were kept. Storms swept the city but, fortunately, there were a few intermittent periods of sunshine to brighten the sombre skies.

1923

On New Year's Day a far-reaching change in industrial life took place when the 300 or so railway companies in Great Britain came to an end and were merged into four great groups.

As far as East Anglia was concerned, the most important aspect of the merger was that the London and North East Railway Company would, in the future, be the name under which the Eastern Group would operate. At Thorpe Station, the travelling public were soon to see LNER painted on all rolling stock.

In the city, Way Down East, featuring Lilian Gish, was being shown for six days at the Haymarket Picture House. Miss Gish was extremely popular and the film was held for a further six days, many people having been turned away by the 'House Full' notice in the first week.

There was more excitement in store after this film closed: the next programme was The Sheik starring Rudolf Valentino. Mothers and daughters queued to see their screen idol.

February

The papers announced the death from cancer of the well known Norwich artist, Miss Catherine Maud Nichols. Her paintings and dry point engravings had earned her an international reputation; she had

Castle Meadow in 1922, before the road was widened.

been a founder member of the Norfolk and Norwich Art Circle, the first president of the Woodpeckers Art Club and the first lady member of the Royal Society of Painters and Etchers. Miss Nichols had had no regular art training. Apart from her artistic abilities, she gave lectures and talked fluently on philosophy and campaigned vigorously against vivisection and other forms of cruelty to animals. Her death robbed the city of one of its loved characters.

In reviewing the existing music, singing and dancing licences in Norwich, the Chief Constable thought it prudent to adjourn the granting of a licence to The Old Spring Gardens, Mountergate, until further public safety requirements could be met.

The Spring Gardens Pavilion had been opened in 1910 when it had been a large, green canvas structure. The stage had been built by Messrs Boulton & Paul and refreshments were supplied by Mr Marchesi of Prince of Wales Road. The Pavilion was situated in large gardens in Mountergate and was one of the city's beauty spots. Shows such as *Brownies, Cigarettes, Scamps, Tatler, Cabaret Killers* (with Ronald Frankon and Nauton Wayne) and *The Chocs* with the then unknown singer Norman Long, were all shown there.

Throughout the twenties, people spent fine evenings watching the shows and, during the intervals, strolling through the fairyland atmosphere provided by the illuminated tree-lined walks or standing under the ancient mulberry tree.

On warm nights, the canvas sides of the pavilion were raised so that as many people as possible could see the show. In later years, the marquee-type theatre was replaced by a plain brick and asbestos building.

Stars who performed there included Leonard Henry, Doris Hare, Leslie Henson and Stanley Holloway. It was even said that Ronald Coleman once appeared there before going to America. The pavilion was also used for dinners and the lovely dresses of the girls added to the colourful, romantic scene.

Jarvis and Sons Ltd of St Benedict's opened in the early 1900s. At that time, the street was overcrowded with shops, but this drapers and furniture shop flourished throughout the 1920s and was to become one of the largest businesses in the city by the 1930s.

St Benedict's was heavily populated by tiny yards which spiked out from its length. They included Queen of Hungary Yard, Reeve's Yard, Bee Hive Yard, Crown Yard, Fountain Yard, Pipe Burners Yard, Turners Court,

Green's Yard, Three Kings Yard, Plough Yard and Adam and Eve Yard.

These colourful names were inscribed on the archways that led down to cobbled yards, down the centre of which often ran open drains. A single

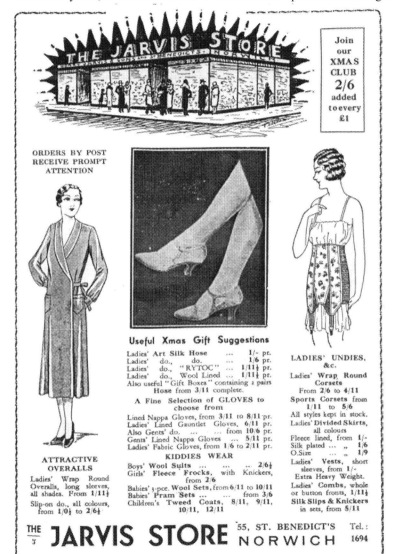

standpipe usually supplied all of the houses in the yard and a row of out-side lavatories added to the slum-like atmosphere.

The government announced that it would provide an annual contribution of £200,000 towards improving slum areas in cities. It was believed that Norwich would be allocated some of this money. Appalling housing conditions were thought to be responsible for much sickness and bad health which caused such large claims on approved societies.

Young boys and girls aged around 16 were coming into these societies year after year, suffering not only from the effects of poor housing but also from malnourishment.

April

Mr Leonard Bolingbroke generously presented The Strangers' Hall to the city and his gift also included his magnificent collection of furniture and bygones. His house was to be opened as a Folk Museum.

June

His Royal Highness the Prince of Wales visited the Royal Norfolk Show in June and, while in Norwich, he also opened the new Carrow Bridge. The old bridge, built in 1810, was constructed of cast iron on wood piles and work on its replacement, a steel bridge, had been started in 1920 as an unemployment work scheme.

On 16 June, Norwich Rose Day, 500 boxes of fresh roses were sold and 100,000 coins collected for charity.

July

The weather this month was magnificent: the temperature reached 82° in Norwich on the 9th, 94° on the 11th, 92° on the 12th and on the 13th it was 89°.

August

The beautiful weather persisted. On Bank Holiday Monday 17,000 day trippers left Thorpe Station for the seaside.

September

During this month, Norwich was linked to London and Manchester by an air service. The Air Ministry had authorised Daimler Airways to run the service. It was thought that passengers would probably arrange their bookings through Mann Egerton's garage, of Prince of Wales Road, who would convey them to the Mousehold Aerodrome.

Another new bridge was opened. As Norwich extended, grappling with the problems of enlarging a mediaeval city to meet modern needs, a new bridge, built of mass concrete piers and faced with concrete blocks, was erected over the new Mile Cross Road.

Old Barge Yard took its name from the Old Barge inn (so named by 1806), now known as Dragon Hall.

October

The Norwich Housing and Home Life Economy Exhibition opened at the Agricultural Hall. Included in the many trade stands were Charles Gates, electrical engineer, who was exhibiting wireless receiving sets.

The Lazar House, just outside the city walls, has been an isolation hospital, a barn, cottages and (from 1923 to 2003) a library. The two Norman doorways and the tiny round windows at the top are original.

Mr G. Valori, of Waterloo Road, had Stand Number 69 where his special ice cream could be sampled, and at Stand 50 Messrs Backs Ltd, the old established firm, supplied their well-known wines, spirits and beers.

Herrings were in good supply in Norwich as the Yarmouth herring season surpassed all hopes. On Saturday 20 October, the crowning point of the season was reached with the colossal catch of 28 million fish (28,000 crans).

November

November saw the opening of Lazar House, Sprowston Road, as a branch library. Lazar House, or Magdalen Chapel, was believed to have been built by Bishop de Losinga around the beginning of the 12th century. The building was restored by the late Sir Eustace Gurney JP in 1907 and presented to the city in 1921. When it opened in 1923 it consisted of a lending department and a separate juvenile library and a reading room.

December

Lloyd George visited Norwich, where he held a meeting at the Hippodrome Theatre, St Giles, before going to the Haymarket Picture House Restaurant for tea.

Miss Dorothy Jewson and Mr W. R. Smith, the Labour candidates, were elected at the local elections.

A very special – and surprising – Christmas present this year was a decrease in the rates of five pence in the pound.

The year ended with the appearance of a real, old-fashioned and picturesque Christmas: the city was covered with snow.

1924

The start of the new year heralded the beginning of the sales in the city's shops. Messrs Chamberlins of Guildhall Hill were selling black artificial hose at one shilling and eleven pence a pair.

They were also advertising ladies' knickers made of jap satin at 8*s* 11*d*. Dress fabrics were also on sale at two shillings a yard for striped serge, reduction in wages would be about seven shillings a week.*

Later in January, sale threatened one of the best-known buildings in Norwich: it was announced that Samson and Hercules House was suitable for use as a factory or similar. Norwich citizens were outraged: the debasement of this fine old building, situated at the very gates of the Cathedral, was unthinkable. Some time earlier, discussions had taken place about starting a first class club in the building if it came onto the market, but this project had fallen through.

It was announced that the House, together with the adjoining Augustine Steward's House, was to be offered for public auction unless financial aid for its preservation was forthcoming.

The wonders of wireless telegraphy were brought to the notice of the general public. Thousands of people were able to hear the speeches of the Prince of Wales and His Majesty the King at the opening of the British Empire Exhibition at Wembley when the Norwich newspaper and Messrs Mann Egerton & Co Ltd arranged for the installation of a loudspeaker in St Andrew's Hall. The Prince of Wales was heard clearly, but the thinning effects of the mechanism seemed to give His Royal Highness a cockney accent.

February

On 9 February a further appeal was launched to stop the sale of the Samson and Hercules, and it was suggested that it could be used as a civic art gallery.

Miss Dorothea Jewson, the MP for Norwich, demonstrated her sympathy with the railwaymen's strike by deciding to boycott trains during the dispute. She announced she would walk home to Norwich from London. The lady Member set out from her flat in Bloomsbury and, though she obtained a few short lifts, the majority of her journey was made on foot. The welcome news that the dispute was over reached her when she arrived at Bury St Edmunds, so Miss Jewson completed her journey to her home at Tower House, Bracondale, by train.

Chamberlins shop on Guildhall Hill. The bunting is for the 1935 Silver Jubilee.

and 54-inch wide fashionable check, all wool fabrics cost 2s 6d a yard. Ladies' coats in grey gabardine were six guineas while brown velour coats trimmed with wool embroidery cost 60 shillings. Messrs Chamberlins had been founded in 1815 and by the 1920s the name Chamberlins of Norwich denoted quality at a reasonable price.

As January drew to a close, a partial railway strike dislocated travel considerably. The problem had arisen over a new award which provided that drivers and firemen, who had been paid extra for all mileage over 120 miles per day,

The Norwich Electric Tramways Company penny stages in the city in 1924 were Eaton Terraces to Eaton Road, Orford Place to Thorpe

A tram at St Benedicts in 1934

parked in Chapel Field Gardens. The tank stayed, despite their disapproval and one member of the Council suggested it should be converted into a rockery.

Norfolk Education Committee became unpopular when people thought it was imposing a ban on marriage, by asking women teachers who got married to resign their posts.

Under the terms of the Cinematography Act 1909, the licences of theatres and cinemas in Norwich had to be reviewed during March. The premises affected included the Assembly House, Agricultural Hall; Empire Theatre, Prince of Wales Road; Hippodrome, St Giles' Street; Cinema Palace, Magdalen Street; Theatre de Luxe, St Andrews Street; Thatched Theatre, All Saints Green; and the Haymarket Picture House, Haymarket.

At the Electric Theatre *The Four Horses of the Apocalypse* was being shown. This was reported as being the masterpiece of the age which deserved to be handed down to future generations. More than 500,000 feet or 95 miles of film was used in its making, the production costs slightly exceeded £250,000 and the cast numbered 12,500. At the Electric, George Benson presented the prologue and an augmented orchestra supplied the music.

May
A clerk who lived in Orchard Street was bound over in the sum of £5 and ordered to pay three shillings costs for betting on a horse at a newsagent's in Westwick Street. The newsagent was fined £60 or 61 days' imprisonment.

July
Costessey Mill was gutted by fire; the first storey was almost completely destroyed and the whole building was a roaring inferno. Sheets of flame poured from every window and a policeman risked his life by crawling through dense smoke to rescue a black and white cat which was imprisoned by the fire.

Among the amenities advertised by the Regent Theatre, Prince of Wales Road, were free garage space and dainty teas and ice creams. Seat prices were 2s 4d, 2s, 1s 6d, 1s 3d, 1s, 8d and 5d.

Station, Dereham Road Terraces to St Benedict's Gates, St Benedict's Gates to Royal Hotel, Stump Cross to Royal Hotel and Magdalen Gates to Tombland.

Norwich trams rearranged their penny stages. On the Dereham Road route, the main penny stage had been from Alexandra Road to Ten Bell Lane, and than had been extended to Charing Cross. In future it was to be from Newmarket Terrace to Orford Place.

March
In the first week of the month, 153 girls employed by Messrs Harmers of St Andrew Street went on strike. During the weekend the girls marched around Norwich carrying banners; stopping occasionally to throw snowballs at each other good naturedly. Their dispute was settled within a week, by payment of increases, varying between sixpence and a shilling a week.

The Council expressed their disapproval of the wartime tank *Lily II* remaining

August

The king's son and his young bride, the Duke and Duchess of York, passed through Norwich on their way to Woodbastwick Hall, the home of Mr and Mrs John Cator. Their daughter, Miss Betty Cator, had been a bridesmaid at the wedding of the royal couple the previous year.

September

The Unemployment Committee reported on additional work to relieve unemployment during the winter months. It was reported that 2,709 men were registered as unemployed. This compared with approximately 5,000 men a year earlier. Works in progress included the reconstruction of Whitefriars Bridge where 20 men were at work; another 20 were employed on the river-widening scheme at Elm Hill, 58 were involved in the creation of a yacht pond at Eaton Park and 30 were engaged on laying out Wensum Park. These schemes and others were helping to alleviate some of the hardship.

The creation of Wensum Park gave employment to 30 men. It remains a pleasant location for rest and recreation today.

The Norwich candidates for the General Election presented their nominations on 18 October. J. Griffyth Fairfax of 68 Bracondale, barrister-at-law, stood in the Conservative interest; Edward Hilton Young of London, Privy Councillor, represented the Liberals and for the Labour Party were Dorothea Jewson, Tower House, Bracondale, official of the National Union of General Workers, and R. W. Smith, Belle Vue, Old Catton, an official of the National Union of Boot and Shoe Operatives.

On the day of the election, 29 October, in the poorer areas of the city – Ber Street, Cowgate, Heigham Street – bands of children tottered along, displaying posters on their backs and beating toffee tins and old saucepans. Even dogs and cats were decorated with party ribbons! It was not until 4 o'clock that the final results were announced, victory going to Hilton Young (Liberal) and Griffyth Fairfax (Conservative).

On the last day of the month, Miss Ethel Mary Colman consented to become Lord Mayor of Norwich. The appointment created a precedent for though women had occupied the office of mayor in many towns and cities in Britain, none had been elected to the higher dignity of Lord Mayor.

October

There were no prisoners for trial at the Autumn Sessions for Norfolk – a state which had been unknown for many years. The only items before the court were an application for the diversion of a cart track and formal appointments of Justices as visitors of public licenced houses.

December

As the year ended, and Christmas advertisements filled the newspapers, people hurrying to do their shopping found they could buy:

> Norfolk turkey, at 1*s* 10*d* and 2*s* per lb
> Christmas puddings at 1*s* 4*d* to 3*s* 6*d*
> Iced Christmas cake at 2*s* to 8*s* 9*d*
> Mincemeat 10*d* to 1*s* 7*d* a jar
> Tunis dates at 8*d* a box
> Figs (loose) at 6*d* per lb
> Pineapple at 7*d* a large tin
> Peaches at 1*s* 0½*d* a large tin

1925

The Secretary of State decided that the practice of keeping a small number of female prisoners at Norwich prison should be discontinued. All female prisoners, whether convicted or not, were to be sent to Holloway Prison. People felt that the Secretary of State should reconsider his decision: great hardship would be caused to prisoners owing to the distance involved, and women not yet convicted would be confined in the company of uniformed officers. It was suggested that arrangements be made with the Committee at St Augustine's Lodge, Lady Lane, for reception in the home of women prisoners on remand, for a charge of five shillings a day, to include meals and a bed.

Norwich City Council and many other bodies were congratulated when another batch of 100 houses on Earlham and Mile Cross Estates were completed, to be let at five shillings a week.

At the Thatched Theatre in the week commencing 5 January a film called *Poisoned Paradise* was shown. It was the forbidden story of Paris and Monte Carlo, made from a book banned by continental police because it told too much. It starred Clara Bow, Raymond Griffiths and Kenneth Harrison.

One of the courts of Norwich, occupying the rear part of a once desirable house but now in a state of decay

If this was too shocking for cinemagoers who wanted only to be entertained, Lou Chaney was starring at the Haymarket in *The Hunchback of Notre Dame*.

In January, the Corporation received a recommendation from the Museum Committee to purchase numbers 10, 12 and 14 Charing Cross, forming part of and adjoining Strangers' Hall, at a cost of £1,500.

The Queen motored from Sandringham to a special service at the Cathedral in January. The service was held to dedicate the work of renovating the ancient episcopal throne, once the seat of Bishop Herbert de Losinga.

February

The appalling condition of so many houses in Norwich was highlighted this month. The Minister of Health would have liked to close 3,000 Norwich houses, which were slowly decaying in the yards and alleyways.

The City Council put forward a scheme for improvements in Robinson Yard in Oak Street. In this area nine yards sloped down from Oak Street to the River Wensum. A high percentage of the houses in the Yards were damp and in most cases the water supply was outside.

Some 217 people lived in 52 houses, all without damp courses; all except one had no sinks, all were some distance from the toilets, and of the 52 houses, 12 had one bedroom, 36 had 2 bedrooms and four had three

bedrooms. The 12 one bedroom houses were occupied by 36 people, 12 of them under 10 years of age. Three cottages in the Yards were served by one toilet closet, while 34 people used another three toilets.

Like so many streets in Norwich, Oak Street was honeycombed by these small yards. They ran, medieval fashion, back from the streets. Their occupants often stood at the entrances, prematurely aged by poverty. The poorly clad women stood chatting, their thin, often deformed children clinging to their black-clad misshapen figures. The entrances to the Yards were the only source of cleaner-smelling air.

Along Oak Street, the following Yard names were recorded:

Dial	White Lion	Suffolk Arms	Tuns
Howman's	Smith's	Saw Mill	Hawkes
Flower Pot	Distillery	Bath House	Holls
Buck's	Ragged School	Little Buck	Unicorn
Key & Castle	Eight Ringers	New Mills	Robinson's
Sun	Queen Caroline	Horton's	Rudd's
Little Qu. Caroline	Sadler's	Arabian Horse	Ltl. Arabian Horse
Osborne's	Fellmongers	Baldwin's	Goat
Dog	Angel	Swan	Talbot
Little Brew	Old Brew	Royal Oak	Greenland Fishery

On 22 February the Norwich Girls High School celebrated its 50th anniversary. At the celebrations were 12 old girls who had been first year students in 1875, including Agnes Buckingham, Maria Colman, Edith Crowe and Beatrice Thorn.

The Queen Caroline in Oak Street closed in February, while in Castle Street the 'Better Ole Club' applied for a music and singing licence, as they had installed a four-valve wireless set. The Queen Victoria in Magdalen Street also went in for this new form of entertainment. With its population of 120,653, Norwich had 484 licensed premises, but even with all these public houses there was very little drunkenness in the city.

June

Norwich gave a great welcome to Prince Henry when he formally opened the new premises of the Norwich Lads Club. The Chief Constable, Mr J. H. Dain, had founded the club in 1918, and as it now had a membership of 6,000 lads over the age of 14, their old premises in St George's Street had become inadequate for their needs.

141 Oak Street: the sign identifies the entrance as leading to Little Buck Yard. Note the windows in the top storey of this former weaver's house, designed to give maximum light for working hand looms.

August

There was a riot in the workhouse in Bowthorpe Road during August. Wearing a red rosette, one of the leaders of the Norwich unemployed appeared in the dock of the Guildhall. He was charged with being a person maintained in the workhouse who unlawfully refused to obey the lawful order of the Workhouse Master.

While exercising in the workhouse yard, he addressed a meeting; when the Master appeared, all the men started to sing the Red Flag. The Master asked him to leave the yard, and he refused to do so. A crowd of about 85 men were hooting and shouting, the police were called, and the man was arrested after a struggle.

Augustine Steward House, carefully restored in the 1990s but preserving its curious angles! ▶

This plaque on Suckling House (now Cinema City) records its occupancy by numerous former City notables. The house was restored in 1923 by Edward Thomas Boardman. ▶▶

The Norfolk and Norwich Archaeological Trust and the local branch of the Young Women's Christian Association came to a joint decision in August to purchase Samson and Hercules House. They invited the public to help by subscribing to a fund which would allow the house to be repaired and equipped as a central club house for women and girls, with opportunities for social, physical and educational activities.

The house on Tombland, and its beautiful neighbour Augustine Steward House, had never lacked publicity. When it had become known two years previously that it was for sale, many suggestions had been proposed for its use. The house is said by Kirkpatrick to have been built by Christopher Jay during his mayoralty in 1657. It was very worrying for people who recalled that, incredibly, in 1829 the Bridewell Museum had almost been sold by the Corporation to a private individual for £1,140, with no conditions as to its preservation.

SUCKLING'S HOUSE
Wm. de Rollesby. 1285
John Fairchild. Bailiff 1331
John Parlet. M.P. Bailiff 1380
John Cambridge. Mayor 1414
John Clerk. M.P. Mayor 1507
Robert Suckling. M.P.
Mayor 1564
LIVED HERE.

The Bridewell was where the first Mayor of Norwich, William Appleyard, kept open house on the occasion of King Henry IV granting Norwich a charter enabling the City to choose its own Mayor, thus separating the city from the county of Norwich.

Suckling and Stuart House, which dates back to the reign of Richard II, was restored and presented to the city by the Misses Colman of Carrow Abbey, Norwich. The house had been occupied by a long series of city notables, including the Suckling family. This gift to the city was to enrich the St Andrew area. First there had been Mr L. G. Bolingbroke's splendid gift of Strangers Hall, then the Bridewell was presented by Mr H. M. Holmes, and now Suckling House. The Misses Colman built a hall capable of holding about 450 people on an adjacent piece of land, as a memorial to their sister, Mrs E. Stuart. This was a very welcome gift as the city was in great need of a well-equipped hall for lectures and demonstrations.

October

After a vigorous debate, the proposal to erect additional County Council offices in Castle Gardens, at the South End, was turned down; it was suggested that a more suitable site should be found.

On Saturday 24 October their Royal Highnesses the Duke and Duchess of York visited Norwich for the centenary celebrations of Norwich Castle Museum. In a very full day, they arrived at the Castle for luncheon then, with the Lord Mayor Dr G. Stevens Pope, they received the deeds of the Bridewell from Mr H. M. Holmes. The Duke opened the new Bridewell Museum of Local Industries. In the afternoon His Highness opened Suckling House and later opened Samson and Hercules House as a YWCA club.

From 26 to 31 October was 'Norwich At Home' week, when the general public had the opportunity to view the city's many activities. The General Post Office, Sorting and Telegraph Department was opened to inspection, as were many boot and shoe factories, the electricity works, Duke Street trams, the gas works, Norwich Mercury companies, printing works, Messrs Jarrolds printing works and the Lads Club, to name but a few. There were rambles through Norwich streets, exhibitions, guides and lectures, and shop windows displayed goods made in Norwich. The week was organised by the Norwich Rotary Club and was a resounding success in spite of general unrest and industrial problems.

Looking down St Andrews Hill: the boarded-up building is Suckling House before its restoration.

November

The death of Queen Alexandra was announced. She had died of a heart attack at the age of 81, while staying at Sandringham. The widespread affection felt for her throughout Norfolk was shown in the many tributes from civic leaders and ordinary people.

December

December saw Norwich Corporation announcing a levy of three shillings in the pound on rates, which was needed for poor relief. It was done with great regret, and with some apprehension for the future.

Some Councillors believed that the money spent on relief was excessive, and that the time had come when a drastic cut should be made. The increase meant that the total rates for this half of the year amounted to ten shillings in the pound.

Unemployment relief was being paid to 729 more people in Norwich than at the same time in the previous year.

On Christmas Day, gloom was forgotten. Norwich City Football Team were playing Crystal Palace, and this had not happened for several years.

Although rail services were cut to the minimum, the LNER was serving Christmas meals on the restaurant cars on trains running on the East Coast route to the North and Kings Cross on Christmas Day.

The luncheon menu included roast goose; the dinner menu featured turkey and Christmas pudding.

1926

The year was heralded by a 50 mph wind.

At the Cathedral, 800 people attended the Watch Night service. In the first week of the year, the Haymarket was showing College Days, starring Harold Lloyd, while at the Theatre de Luxe, St Andrew's, the special attraction was Gloria Swanson in The Wages of Fear.

In the local paper, passages to Canada were being advertised at a cost of only £3 to approved applicants; many people began to think that emigration might be the only answer to bad housing and lack of employment. 'Notes on Canada' was the title of a feature appearing regularly in the local paper.

The state of some housing in Norwich was brought into sharp focus in the first week of January when a house collapsed in Baker's Yard, Barrack Street. There were 22 people living in the small four-roomed house but miraculously none was hurt. As the gable suddenly began to bulge, some of the occupants had run out into the street, shouting to others to run for their lives.

Meanwhile, a circular from Whitehall was received in Norwich saying that in future local authorities would be given grants only if there was abnormal unemployment, and the only work which qualified was work which otherwise would not be undertaken for at least five years.

It was feared that Norwich would become the most heavily rated County Borough in England in order to meet the poor law costs of workless men and women. Relief works to the value of £137,000 had already been approved by Norwich Council, and part of this sum had already been spent.

February

A bullock on Chamberlin's Meadow, Ipswich Road, was found to be infected with foot and mouth disease. An absolute standstill order was imposed within a seven-mile radius of the Ipswich Road, and an Infected Order was declared within a radius of 15 miles of Norwich.

March

Lively scenes occurred on the Market Place in March when the Norwich Area of the British Union of Fascists organised a meeting. About 1,000 people listened to the speeches, interrupting freely and frequently. The meeting began with the Union Jack being raised; one woman speaker was heckled so severely that she had to sit down. At the end of the meeting, the crowd was invited to sing the National Anthem. Many did so, but a section of the crowd began singing the Red Flag. The meeting got completely out of hand, and the police had to escort the speakers from the Market Place.

On 27 March the Theatre Royal celebrated its centenary. The new Theatre Royal was opened on 27 March 1826 with a programme of *School for Scandal* and *Youth, Love and Folly.*

May

May Day saw a huge crowd gathered in the Market Place as Norwich Labour and Trade Union organisations assembled in their thousands, with bands and banners. The General Strike loomed.

On 3 May the incredible happened. The County was gripped by a General Strike. By 5 May the *Eastern Evening News* was being published as one sheet of paper, printed on just one side. Copies of the government's emergency publication, *The British Gazette*, had been received in Norwich for local sale, but pickets prevented their sale until they had held a meeting. The *Eastern Daily Press* was brought out as a foolscap typed sheet.

Postal, telephone and telegraph services were congested, and users were asked to keep their messages short.

Although a few trains were still getting through to Thorpe Station, tram services in the city were at a standstill.

Supplies of eggs and farm produce were abundant in Norfolk, and milk was in ample supply at 3*d* a pint. Messrs Caley & Son Ltd of Chapel Field Road announced they would be closing.

In shoe factories, the order of the day was that those people still working were not to use more than 50% of the fuel consumed during the four weeks immediately preceding the strike.

Mr Herbert Gowen, Chairman of the Norwich Volunteer Service, which had its headquarters at the Agricultural Hall, said there had been more volunteers than there was work for them.

During the first week, all the builders joined the strike, and all transport men in Norwich were called out. People gathered around the windows of the *Norwich Mercury* office, where the latest wireless bulletins were displayed to the excited crowd.

It was said that 3,000 workers were idle in Norwich and it was feared that if the strike continued 20,000 people would be out. The breweries, anticipating the strike of their draymen, had made large deliveries to all their public houses.

Fish was rapidly disappearing from the menus of local hotels, but there was great rejoicing when a train got through from Lowestoft. Commercial travellers were making city calls only, having given up the attempt to get out into the county. The staff of local shops stayed loyal to their employers in the main.

As the days went on, the trade unionists at Keir Hardie Hall decided to counteract rumours by issuing a daily bulletin. By 9 May the shoe factories were posting notices that half hire only was to be worked because of the shortage of electrical power.

By the second week of the strike, the police in Norwich were thankful that no serious trouble had occurred, although there had been many small incidents, such as the occasion when women and strikers hissed at a clerk who delivered lorry-loads of beer to a restaurant in White Lion Street.

The tramway men took the view that omnibuses should not be allowed to run on tram routes. Pickets were accordingly stationed on Newmarket Road and other routes; this occasioned many lively exchanges!

In general, Norwich managed to carry on in an orderly fashion, in spite of the creeping paralysis throughout its factories.

On 10 May newspapers reported that only about one-third of the normal number of cattle had arrived at the cattle market sale. These cattle had walked through strangely silent streets to the Castle Hill sale ground.

Two days later, the TUC met the Prime Minister, and it was announced that the General Strike had collapsed. At shortly after 10am on the next day, Norwich tram men returned to work and by midday a full service was operating. Norwich resumed its industrial life.

Cattle driven to the market occasionally wandered! Two beasts are seen here in June 1937 in the Browne garden on Hay Hill, beside St Peter Mancroft church.

At a time when the nation was preoccupied with the consequences of the General Strike, Messrs Colman created a classic advertising campaign. They devised the Mustard Club. A prospectus was issued in the press and the faces of special characters, devised by the artist John Gilroy, filled the pages. A badge was offered to members, and a special department of ten girls was created to deal with the 2,000 membership applications received each day. Eight Mustard Club songs and card games were published. Also published were booklets with copy written by Dorothy L. Sayers and Robert Bevan, which were eagerly purchased by the public. For the first time, 98 out of every 100 people seemed to be talking about mustard and, what was more important, talking about mustard that had been made in Norwich.

THE OFFICERS OF THE MUSTARD CLUB
Back Row :- Lord Bacon of Cookham, Master Mustard, Signor Spaghetti
Front Row :- Miss Di Gester (*Secretary*), The Baron de Beef (*President*), Lady Hearty

July

A great Norwich pageant was planned for July. It was to be produced by Nugent Monck, of Maddermarket fame. The venue was Newmarket Road where the ground had been completely transformed: there were 2,300 covered seats, free parking for 1,200 cars, and it was hoped that over 1,000 performers would take part. The pageant had three objects: firstly, it was to promote Norwich as a pleasure resort for visitors; secondly, it should educate the inhabitants of city and county in their history, and finally it should promote the memory of past citizens. Mr Nugent Monck's pageant was a great success, enjoyed by adults and children alike.

The Theatre Royal underwent a renovation in July when its foyer was enlarged to more than three times its original size. The new walls widened into a recess at the back and front of the roof, the auditorium was provided with new seating, and a new electric control switchboard was installed by the Corporation. The theatre reopened with a revue called *The Red Hat*.

September

Resentment against the heavy rate burden in the city continued to grow. General opinion held that there was a considerable waste of public money. There were complaints that the streets were full of potholes and the dustmen never called on a regular day, amongst other things.

Manufacturers could not cut their operating costs because of these increasing overheads, and there was a general cry for the rates to be reduced as soon as possible.

One aspect of Corporation services not criticised was the tramway and bus system which covered the city. The service schedule was:

Eaton and Cavalry Barracks (Colour, Green): Every 12 mins up to 10 a.m., then every 10 mins to 7.40 p.m., then 12 mins to finish. First through cars 7.54 a.m. Saturdays 10 mins to finish.

Earlham and Thorpe Roads (Colour, Red): Every 10 mins up to 8.30 a.m. then every 7½ mins to 7 p.m., then every 10 mins to finish. First through cars from Earlham Road 7.04 a.m., from Thorpe 7.18 a.m. Saturdays 7½ mins to finish.

Unthank and Magdalen Roads (Colour, White): Every 7½ mins up to 8.30 a.m., then every 6 mins up to 12 noon, then every 5 mins to 7 p.m., then 6 mins to finish. First through cars from Magdalen Road 6.34 a.m., from Unthank Road 7.04 a.m.

Dereham Road and Royal Hotel (Colour, Blue): Every 10 mins up to 12 o'clock, then every 7½ mins to 7.15 p.m., then every 10 mins to finish. First through cars from Royal Hotel 7.10 a.m., from Dereham Road 7.25 a.m.

Trowse Station and Orford Place (Colour, Orange): Every 30 mins up to finish. First car from Orford Place 7.45 a.m.; from Trowse 8 a.m.

City Road and Orford Place (Colour, Yellow and Red): Every 30 mins up to finish. First car from Orford Place 8 a.m., from City Road 8.15 a.m.

On Sundays no cars ran before 10 a.m.

Last cars: Weekdays from Orford Place to Trowse 10.15 p.m., to City Road 10.30 p.m., to Cavalry Barracks, Newmarket Road 10.45 p.m., to Unthank Road, Earlham Road, Thorpe Road 10.45 p.m., to Magdalen Road 11.10 p.m., to Aylsham Road from St Andrew's Church 10.30 p.m., to Dereham Road from Royal Hotel 10.45 p.m.

December
On Christmas Day there was a football match between the Canaries and Brentford. Kick-off was at 11.15 a.m.

1927
A number of very popular films were being shown in Norwich in the first week of the year. At the Theatre de Luxe Ronald Coleman was appearing in *The Dark Angel*; the Haymarket was showing *The Black Pirate* starring Douglas Fairbanks; and Dorothy Gish was portraying the orange girl in *Nell Gwynne*, at the Regent, Prince of Wales Road.

Meanwhile, the city stores were full of people rushing to obtain a bargain at the sales. Messrs Bunting Stores at the corner of Rampant Horse Street placed a four-page advertisement in the Norwich Journal for their many sale items. Included were hem stitched, pure linen sheets at 23s 9d a pair, Axminster carpets, 13 ft 6 ins x 10 ft 6 ins, at £8 15s, felt and wool pull-on hats at 2s, all wool ladies' two-piece suits, with matching dress, 30s, and children's gloves at 1s a pair.

Not to be outdone, at their All Saints' Green shop Bonds announced their stocktaking sale. They were selling full size mattresses at 21s, striped Turkish towels for only 1s with odd sizes at 6d, umbrellas at 2s 9d and artificial silk hose at 2s.

Moores of St Benedict's also joined in the sales battle of local shops.

A tram makes its way through Orford Place.

The industrial outlook in Norwich was changing, with a revival anticipated. Optimism prevailed throughout the boot and shoe trade and, with the coal strike over, coal was being produced on a more economical basis which helped most factories.

Mr S. Delves, of Delves Motors Ltd, Rose Lane and Prince of Wales Road, said most people in his trade had been running down their stock throughout 1926; hopes for more orders, though, heralded better prospects for 1927.

Mr J. Walter Bunting, Director of Chamberlin's on Guildhall, said that in the past month or two they had received many more orders in their clothing factory than in the previous year. All-round optimism was the order of the day.

A tablet was unveiled in the Cathedral in memory of the late Bishop of Thetford. Cast in bronze, it was the work of a local art student, Miss Maidie Buckenham.

*Aero enthusiasts
at Mousehold*

Norwich City Council unanimously approved a proposal that President Lincoln's ancestral association with Norfolk should be commemorated by a statue in Norwich. The *Eastern Daily Press* suggested that the only motive was to attract American tourists to the city. The newly formed Norfolk Pilgrim Society decided to issue a circular to their members designed to raise funds so as to ensure a worthy memorial to Abraham Lincoln was erected.

A big demolition programme was under way in the heart of the city in preparation for rebuilding. Lloyds Bank were erecting a new bank on the Walk, and Messrs Barclays were building fine new premises.

One of the most ambitious schemes was that of the Norwich Union Fire Assurance building in Surrey Street. Further big extensions were being carried out by Messrs W. H. H. Clarke in Northumberland Street, the Norfolk and Norwich Hospital had built a new children's block the previous year, and a new outpatients' block was nearing completion. Norwich looked to the future with renewed hope.

February

A public meeting was held in Blackfriars Hall in February, with the aim of forming a Norwich Aero Club. When the aims of the Club were explained, Mr Henry N. Holmes and Mr James Hardy promised to give the club a Moth aeroplane. An instructor was to be engaged, and a hangar, office and the services of a ground engineer were loaned by Messrs Boulton and Paul.

With one aircraft, the club began its active career in the early summer of 1927 and was able to claim the distinction of being the first light aeroplane club to be promoted by the municipality's civic leaders.

There were many rumours of transformation schemes in Orford Place, and considerable improvement was already in progress. The tram corner had been completely altered, with a modern structure erected to provide a wider space for the benefit of both pedestrians and traffic.

It is an ill wind that blows nobody good, and a disastrous fire which

Eastern Daily Press

468.—REGISTERED FOR TRANSMISSION AS A NEWSPAPER.   NORWICH, FRIDAY, JANUARY 7, 1927.   THREE HALF-P

devastated a builder's yard in Chapel Field Road resulted in the yard being replaced by the Dunlop Company with a new building.

An aerial pageant was held on Mousehold Heath, with clubs from all over the country sending machines to support the Light Aeroplane Club of Norwich. Bircham Newton aerodrome sent planes and No 7 squadron from Andover performed alongside contenders from Newcastle-on-Tyne, Lancashire and Yorkshire. There was no charge for admission to the event.

May

Norwich held a Norfolk Eisteddfod in May, with four of the largest halls – St Andrew's, Blackfriars, Martineau and Stuarts – fully utilised each day. The musical competition attracted 2,600 competitors.

June

An old crypt was discovered at 49 St Stephens Street: in the course of alterations to the premises of Mr Sydney Duncan a shallow room was found beneath the shop, which at one time had been used for domestic purposes. On a lower level was a smaller room loosely filled with rubble. Careful excavations revealed a 14th-century crypt.

Herbert Witard

July

The Norfolk and Norwich Hospital reported a rise in the number of accidents due to increased motor traffic.

Cheaper and simpler wirelesses were being promised as more and more people acquired these wonderful receivers. The newest sets could now be made without aerials, and short wave reception was to be improved.

October

After several years' delay, Norwich's Civic War Memorial was unveiled, in the presence of one of the biggest crowds ever seen in the city. The people assembled to honour the 3,544 men of the city who gave their lives in the 1914–18 war.

November

Alderman Herbert E. Witard became the first Labour Lord Mayor of Norwich. After leaving school at the age of 12, Mr Witard had waited two years and then gone as cabin boy on a fishing smack. He came back to Norwich two years later and started work in the boot trade, where he remained for a number of years, not entering the world of politics until the turn of the century. In 1903 he joined the Council and served on most of the important committees.

December

As Christmas approached, the most important matter under discussion by the City Council was the provision of houses at Lakenham. They were negotiating to purchase 73,257 acres of land, owned by Major S. W. Trafford and Wroxham Estate Ltd, about a mile from the city centre approached by City Road and Hall Road. The City Engineer had prepared a layout plan for the erection of approximately 630 houses on 63 acres, with the remaining land to be used as allotments, playing fields, open spaces, etc.

Over the Christmas period the Council referred to committee the petition signed by 6,000 Norwich people calling attention to the desirability of granting free travel facilities to blind people living in the city.

Christmas week saw a new Secondary School for girls rapidly nearing completion at St Clement's Hill, while on the Market Place the ancient and picturesque Fishmongers Arms public house was being demolished.

The Norfolk and Norwich Hospital opened its new outpatients' department. It was part of an extensive scheme which had been in operation for two or three years, and the approximate cost of the new department was £23,000. A bronze relief sculpture of William Fellows, the founder in 1771, was placed on the outside wall. It was the work of the young Norwich sculptress Miss Maidie Buckenham.

The Transformation Schemes being created on the immediate outskirts of the city were a wonderful Christmas present for Norwich. On land which until recently had been open fields now stood 1,802 fine new houses, wide open roads, and playing fields. They had been built within the city boundary by public and private enterprises.

1928

During the first weekend of the New Year, hundreds of local people enjoyed winter sports. There was tobogganing wherever there was a good slope, such as St James' Hill and Cavalry Barracks to the bottom of Kett's Hill. With most of the Broads frozen over and providing miles of ice, there were skaters out on the river at Thorpe. The traditional winter landscape was broken up by a thaw at Hickling Broad on the Sunday night, and there was flooding in the Yare and Wensum valleys.

By the middle of the week the floods assumed serious proportions. On Wednesday night considerable anxiety was caused by the rapid rise of the river Wensum, which flooded the yards around Oak Street.

There was an even more serious cause for anxiety later in the month, when it was learnt that the danger of smallpox spreading to Norfolk was becoming a reality. It had already reached Ely.

February

There were many unvaccinated children in the city, and so fears were well grounded. By the beginning of February it was reported that a mild form of the disease was spreading in the county; tramps were one cause of the spread. By the third week of the month seven cases of smallpox had been

notified by Norwich Poor Law Infirmary.

A great controversy sprang up during the month over the proposed opening of cinemas on Sunday. Those against the proposal argued that the great national heritage of English Sundays was treasured by the vast majority of the citizens of Norwich.

February saw the opening of the handsome new premises of Lloyds Bank on the Walk, and the closure of their London Street premises.

March

At their annual meeting in March, the Friends of the Museum reviewed their purchases for the Castle Museum during 1927. These included, among many other items, a pair of glass decanters engraved 'Norwich a Port c1825' and a pottery statuette of Joseph John Gurney (1788–1847).

April

During April, the City Council discussed its proposed spending of half a million pounds on schemes to help the workless people of Norwich. They included widening Farrow Road, Earlham Road, Old Palace Road and Heigham Street, and building new roads from Philadelphia Lane to Aylsham Road and from Hall Road to Martineau Lane. The Council had approved these schemes but the Ministry of Transport stated funds were not presently available.

Some Council members thought the government largely at fault; they were not prepared to make grants for schemes other than road works, and the government was thought to be callous at a time when 5,000 Norwich men were walking the streets. The government maintained that there was no exceptional unemployment in the city.

May

On 30 May His Royal Highness The Prince of Wales visited Norwich. His primary purpose was to open the magnificent playing fields to be called Eaton Park, but he managed to crowd many other engagements into his four-hour stay. The official timetable read:

11.20   Inspecting the Thorpe Station Yard Guard of Honour of the 4th Battalion Norfolk Regiment T.A.

11.30   Inspecting the new power station.

11.55   Visit homes built at Mousehold in memory of the 6,000 officers and men of the Norfolk Regiment who fell in the war.

12.15   Arrive at Norwich Aerodrome to inspect the aeroplanes of the Norfolk and Norwich Aero Club, to be received by the Club Chairman, Captain A. A. Rice.

12.30   Arrive at Guildhall to be conducted to the Mayor's Parlour by the Lord Mayor, Mr Witard.

12.45   Luncheon

1.33   Lay wreath on the War Memorial outside the Guildhall.

1.37   Arrive at St Andrew's Hall to lay foundation stone of the new Masonic building.

2.10   Walk through the wards of the Jenny Lind Hospital for Children, Unthank Road.

2.32   Inspect members of the British Legion in South Park Avenue.

2.37   Arrive at Eaton Park, to be received by Councillor W. E. Walker, Chairman of the Parks and Gardens Committee.

3.23   Depart for London by train from Thorpe Station.

The Norwich power station at Thorpe

The Norwich Power Station was a notable example of municipal enterprise to show His Highness. In 1893 the first electricity undertakings in the city had been started by a company under the chairmanship of Mr F. W. Harmer, and the generating station was erected at Duke Street. The supply at first was direct current, but in 1913 alternating current generation was adopted. The undertaking was purchased by the Corporation in 1902. In 1922, because of the full capacity of the buildings, the Corporation decided to build a new station. The Thorpe site was purchased and the new power station opened in 1926.

June

The biggest fire for some time occurred in June, destroying the St George's Street premises of Messrs Gunton Sons and Dyball, wholesale ironmongers. There was a great danger of the flames spreading to other premises in the congested area, but the Fire Brigade brought the blaze under control.

During the month the LNER advertised cheap holiday trips to Great Yarmouth. The train left Thorpe Station at 2.30 p.m. and the journey cost 1s 6d. There were also half-day trips to London for 6s.

The month saw another Royal visit to Norwich, when the Duke of Gloucester attended the Royal Norfolk Show at Crown Point.

July

Norfolk was again in the grip of a trade depression. The Lord Mayor called a conference to consider the abnormally high unemployment figures.

The city at this period had a wide range of industries, including foundries and engineering works, iron and wire fence works, brewing, brick works, chemical works, tanneries and the production of mustard, starch and malt vinegar, crêpe, gauze and lace; and there were large boot and shoe factories.

Two thousand shoe operatives were idle, a contributory factor in the slump in the boot and shoe industry being the designs of ladies' fashions in which Norwich specialised. They were very simple, and involved much less manual labour than the more ornate styles which had been fashionable.

An autogiro, familiarly known as a windmill plane, gave a demonstration of its flying capabilities at Mousehold aerodrome in July, causing many an eyebrow to be raised.

Norwich at this period was still a significant manufacturing centre.

August

There was a unique exhibition of a living artist's work at the Castle Museum in August: the work of A. J. Munnings, who was born at Mendham in the Waveney Valley and had been apprenticed to Norwich lithographic printers Page Bros, was on show. The exhibition occupied two corridors and the galleries of the Castle. The opening ceremony was preceded by a luncheon given by the Lord Mayor and Museum Committee.

Some interesting figures on drunkenness were published: they showed that while the number of convictions for drunkenness throughout England and Wales had decreased since the previous year, the number of convictions in Norwich showed a marked increase. The Secretary of the Brewers' Society commented that he felt so far as Norwich being the bottom of the list, it had slightly improved on last year.

September

At the beginning of September it was announced that an enormous amount of the work on building the great airship, the R101, was to be carried out in Norwich. The framework was made at the works of Boulton and Paul. Their contribution represented three-quarters of the total construction work of the ship.

Throughout 1928 discussion continued on the desperate need for new municipal offices. Up to mid 1927 the Corporation's work was carried out in 15

The R101, pride of Boulton & Paul's development engineers

separate buildings. The City Engineer's staff was housed on three floors in a very inconvenient manner.

The police and fire brigade were accommodated in five separate buildings and the City Accountant's staff was housed in three separate buildings. The Health and Sanitary Departments were separated, the former having taken over Sir Peter Eade's old house in St Giles and the latter occupying the Municipal Offices, Market Place.

During the preceding few years the City Fathers had devoted their attention to acquiring property in the vicinity of St Peter's Street, with the eventual aim of building a new City Hall.

December

With the passing of the year, a transformation was taking place along Gentleman's Walk and throughout the city.

The shop of F. Lambert (tea merchant) and H. Samuel (jeweller) in The Walk had undergone a complete transformation: while the reconstructed jewellery shop remained, the rest of the extensive building was converted into an up-to-date Lyons tea shop.

The Norfolk and Norwich Savings Bank had moved to Surrey Street; considerable interior improvements had been carried out at Curl's in Rampant Horse Street, involving the opening of refreshment rooms, while at

Chapel Field Road a new milk depot and model dairy had been opened by the Norwich Co-operative Society. Castle Meadow had been widened to relieve traffic congestion and St Giles was rapidly developing into a modern shopping centre.

The feared smallpox outbreak had not materialised to any significant degree: the highest figure reported by newspapers was 21 cases.

Christmas Day was mild and in London, Boxing Day was the warmest since 1882.

Norwich waited for 1929 with a feeling of hopeful expectancy.

1929

In the first week of the New Year the Haymarket Cinema was showing Charlie Chaplin in *The Circus*. The second feature was *Further Adventures of the Collegians*, and the Haymarket Orchestra and Joan Bullen in a dancing fantasy, *A Dream of New Year* completed the programme.

The directors of the picture house invited poor children to attend a special performance and 650 children took up the invitation. In all over 20,000 people saw the film in five working days.

The Aero Club at Mousehold had three machines of interest to the Norwich public. During the month flights of two hours, covering 140 miles, were to take place, promising a fine view of Norfolk. The flights were available for three people at a time, at an inclusive price of £4 4s 0d.

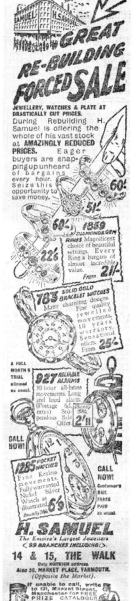

◄◄ *The old Fire Station at 12, Pottergate, in 1936.*

A meeting was held at Suckling House when Judge C. Herbert Smith addressed the National Council of Women on the question: 'What influence will the new women electors exercise on the future legislation?' He thought there had been a lot of claptrap talked for years on the superiority or inferiority of the sexes!

Later in the week, the author Mr F. E. Bailey was reported in the *Eastern Evening News* as saying: 'Women have not learned to think. They have minds like children.'

On Saturday 12 January cup-tie fever was raging in Norwich. What was thought to be the greatest football match ever in the city was to be played between the amateur club The Corinthians and Norwich City. Unprecedented scenes were witnessed as crowds in their thousands lined up outside the ground.

At Thorpe Station, seven excursion trains arrived heavily laden, and people started arriving at the Nest at ten o'clock. By one o'clock, when the gates opened, there were 3,000 people waiting and, as the factory hooters sounded, there was a rush to The Nest. A rough estimate of the crowd was reckoned to be 20,000. Sadly, Norwich were outclassed by the Corinthians, who were the only amateur team left in the Cup. The score was Corinthians 5 Norwich 0.

A strip of land was taken from the corner of Heigh Hall to widen Heigham Street, as part of a street widening scheme. In addition to city road widening, many suburban roads were planned as part of the unemployment relief scheme.

One suggestion then under consideration was that the Cattle Market should be moved from Castle Mound to Harford Estate, with the old site being used for a car park and extension to Castle Gardens. A strong plea for its removal was made by Miss Ethel Colman. She spoke often of the fear and suffering of the cattle when they were driven and jostled along the narrow streets of Norwich on their way to the Cattle Market.

February

Plans for building a new store for Woolworth's in Rampant Horse Street were brought out in February.

The coldest day of the century was recorded in the second week of the month.

Woolworth's new building in Rampant Horse Street

The maximum temperature in Norwich did not exceed 24.5°F on the eleventh. As the afternoon wore on, the thermometer fell still further and by three o'clock it stood at 22.1°. By 15 February the Eastern Evening News reported that Norwich was one of the coldest spots in Britain.

A vessel frozen on the River Yare had to use a breeches buoy to get the crew ashore. Wherries practically disappeared from the rivers; they were unable to sail in such conditions. By the 16th of the month, as tugs were fighting to keep the Yare open, new pack ice was being formed at Berney Arms.

The tugs Mustard Pot, Jeanie Hope, Genstream and Opal broke the ice barrier at Reedham, but big lumps of ice floated downstream to Berney Arms. By 18 February the worst was over: after 176 hours of frost, signs of thaw were apparent in the centre of Norwich.

The ban on broadcasting from music halls was withdrawn on 26 February and people were able to listen to excerpts from the London Coliseum programme.

The Chief Constable of Norwich, Mr J. H. Dain, reported that there were 143 registered aliens in Norwich. The numbers were:

Italians 59	Swiss 11	Chileans 2	Norwegian 2
Belgian 32	Dutch 10	Danish 2	Egyptian 1
French 18	American 9	Japanese 2	Polish 1
German 12	Russian 8	Letts 2	Spanish 1

The sensation of the century was announced at the Haymarket: TALKING FILMS IN NORWICH! The first 'talkie' starred Al Jolson and Sonny Boy in *The Singing Fool*. Talking films had been screened for some months in London, but this was a first for Norwich.

By the end of the month, the arctic weather returned and there were ice packs impeding the traffic on the Yare again. There was a genuine fear that the river would be closed if the frost continued, and this would have meant a coal shortage for the city.

The tugs again encountered heavy ice packs between Reedham and Berney Arms, but still managed to force their way through. It was now possible to skate from Hickling to Heigham Sounds, a distance of some two miles, and conditions were such that if the frost continued for one more night the river would be closed.

Ice yachts were sailing round the Broads, reaching 40 miles per hour in the intensely cold winds. A temperature of 21.2°F was recorded at the meteorological station in Norwich.

By the end of the month the temperature had started to rise and better weather prospects were forecast.

March
March saw the opening of the Blyth Secondary School, Constitution Hill, by the Principal of Newnham College Cambridge.

July
Extensions to the Haymarket Picture House were made in July, adding 500 seats. This brought the total seating capacity to 1,680.

The traffic problems in Norwich were discussed by the City Council during the month. The establishment of a municipal bus service was proposed, but there was already a company, the United Bus Company, that ran a regular service into the city and around the boundaries. There was concern that the establishment of a fleet of municipal buses would cause warfare between private and public companies.

Another small outbreak of smallpox was reported, of the alastrim type. Eight cases occurred in the infants' department of Wensum View School, Waterworks Road, and though the school was not closed the medical officer visited daily.

August
This month saw the opening of a new branch of Messrs Ridley of Ipswich and Bury St Edmunds, in London Street.

A full programme of talking films was to be shown at the Electric Theatre, Prince of Wales Road, from August Bank Holiday onwards. A mechanical orchestra was also being installed. The first big talking picture to be shown was *Lucky Boy*.

September
Pedestrians and motorists stared with interest at the automatic road traffic signals erected at the top of St Stephen's Street.

Norwich businessmen and financiers were outraged when the Bank Rate was raised to 6½% in September: this was its highest level for eight years.

October
The giant R101 airship was completed this month and was granted its permit to fly. Boulton and Paul had contributed girder work regarded as a revelation; they had taken a leading role in aeronautical research and construction over many years, but thought of this project as of unequalled scientific importance. The ship was to carry 100 passengers along with a crew of 50.

Magdalen Street in May 1935. The shops at the left hand side are occupied by Loose's – still there today, though with a new shop front.

Norwich motor car showrooms displayed the latest in motor cars to coincide with this year's Motor Show at Olympia. H. E. Hall & Co of 110 Prince of Wales Road displayed their new Singer Six, priced at £273.

Messrs Howes & Son Ltd, Chapel Field Road and 82–84 Prince of Wales Road, had Stand 100 at the Show; their exhibit comprised a special 20hp 6-cylinder Armstrong Siddeley, chassis price £895. Mauds, of 108 Prince of Wales Road, who were established in 1905, had the Wolseley range, including the new country model de luxe at £450 + £15 tax and the Standard Saloon at £405 + £16 tax.

One of the most elegant stores in Norwich in 1929 was Loose's, where customers could browse along their 100-foot glass-roofed arcade, decorated by a magnificent old vine and ferns and plants of all descriptions. Here were exhibited all that was beautiful in china, glass and earthenware.

The business was thought to have been established in 1791 when the French revolution was shocking the world. Arranged on the shop's shelves were Aynsley and Bisto china; Jasper, Wedgwood, Doulton and Mason ironstone ware; Royal Doulton, Minton and Bretby behind the arcade at the rear; oxidised ware curbs, Companion sets and flower vases. Goods could be bought here and then sent all over Britain as well as abroad. The finest of British wares were displayed proudly.

November

On 1 November the R101 flew over Boulton and Paul: the crowds in the streets had a splendid view, but the greatest thrill was reserved for the employees of Boulton and Paul. At the sound of a hooter, 1,500 of them turned out to greet the magnificent vessel. Although it appeared to be travelling slowly, and flying low, she was actually 3,000 feet high and going at over 60 miles an hour.

Emotions were still strong after 11 years as vast crowds assembled at the War Memorial on Remembrance Day. People left their shop counters and crowded at the windows, balconies and rooftops as the clocks pointed to 11 o'clock. The castle gun boomed, the flag at the Guildhall fell in salute, and an instant silence descended over the crowd.

Not for many years had a new fashion created such widespread interest as when short skirts were replaced by long ones in November 1929. As the leading manufacturing centre for ladies' shoes, Norwich had a particular interest. If skirts were to cover shoes, the beautiful creations of the Norwich factories might not be in such universal demand.

December

The time seemed ripe to consider substituting a bus service for the track tramway service in the city. One City Councillor, Mr F. C. Jex, said he thought buses were infinitely superior to trams; working people, too, seemed to prefer buses.

Despite a period of heavy rain in the run up to Christmas, Christmas Day itself was bright and cheerful and many people took advantage of the weather to walk before settling down to lunch. The golf links in the city also attracted a good number of players.

At the Nest football ground, 11,000 people saw Norwich City defeat Queens Park Rangers by three goals.

The city had a number of hopes and aims for the New Year: one was to see cleaner streets. People were urged to make a real effort to avoid untidiness. In particular, there were three things thought to be vital: first, visitors should be welcomed with a large car park; secondly, trams should be removed from the crowded streets, and thirdly, the street lighting should be improved.

1930

On the first night of the New Year, those Norwich citizens who owned wireless sets received the first regular daily weather forecasts.

Despite its aim to become a cleaner city, Norwich did not have litter baskets, nor were its trams and buses fitted with receptacles for used tickets. Market traders were criticised for their utter disregard for tidiness. Visitors, it was thought, could not get a worse view of the amenities than seeing the flood of waste paper lying in the streets.

In the second week of the month a series of boxing tournaments were held at Norwich Corn Hall in Exchange Street. The principal fight was a six-round contest between Jack Forster of Norwich, the local middleweight champion, and Bill O'Brian of Chicago.

The old 1914–18 wartime tank which stood in Chapel Field Gardens was dismantled. The scrap was purchased by Messrs G. E. Harrison & Son Ltd of Mountergate, scrap iron merchants.

Messrs Cranbox Ltd of Westwick Street, the manufacturers of Odol toothpaste, became one of the first firms in the world to employ the telegraph for transmission of commercial photographs. They received a photograph from their old works in Dresden, Germany, of the 100 millionth bottle of Odol made there. The photograph was received at the London Post Office, and sent from there to Norwich by express letter.

January saw the opening of a new dance hall. The temporary canvas structure at the Spring Gardens was turned into a permanent structure with a maple floor accommodating 500 people. Chinese lanterns were dimmed when the spotlights came into play in the auditorium. The dance music was provided by Percy Cohen and his Haymarket Orchestra.

February

Unemployed workers were employed in the construction of a new bridge over the railway line between Martineau Lane and Hall Road in February. They were paid £2 12s 6d for a 47½-hour week. They started work at 7 o'clock in the morning and finished at 5 o'clock at night. With so many people unemployed, the men were happier with this than being idle.

In spite of the unemployment level, Chief Constable Mr J. H. Dain was very optimistic about the crime figures in the city. A decrease of 96 crimes had been recorded compared to the previous year, and Mr Dain continued his policy of administering a caution to people who were reported for minor crimes.

Norwich was one of the first cities in England to adopt the police telephone system and this, according to the Chief Constable, was helping to fight crime.

Bethel Street in 1930

In the first week of the month Joe Davis, the billiards champion, paid a two day visit to Norwich; it was the first time he had come to the city. Over the two days, his best break was 247, and he made many other breaks over 100.

Sitting at a meeting of the General Purpose Committee at the Castle Museum, the City Council considered plans of the proposed layout for a new municipal office which had been prepared by Mr Robert Atkinson FRIBA. Agreement to the proposed layout was carried unanimously. Mr Atkinson said he thought the building would dominate the city, and thought that a clock tower with a chime of bells would be good value for money.

March

Messrs Garlands, London Street, purchased the shop at 19 London Street which had been Godfrey's. Since the beginning of the year it had practically been rebuilt. Mr Garland had come to Norwich in 1862 from Stroud, Gloucester, and established a drapery shop at 13–17 London Street. His business had expanded over the years and had taken over the corner site, Number 13. The alterations were complete and an opening with a pageant of fashion was held in celebration.

April

This month saw the Lord Mayor walking down Magdalen Street after officially opening Shopping Week. He spoke in praise of the street: it was easy to call it a middle class thoroughfare, he said, but that was only the view of those who did not know from personal experience what a large and varied collection of shops and what an excellent selection of goods were to be found along the street.

During the second week of April the Electric Theatre in Prince of Wales Road was showing the first Cockney talkie, featuring comedians Long and Short as Bill and Alf. There was also a silent feature starring Monty Banks, called Adam's Apple.

At eight o'clock every night the Spring Gardens Theatre presented vaudeville entertainment. The theatre had been further improved and additional comforts had been installed. During the summer months a carefully selected series of concert parties changed each week.

May

The idea of making Norwich a recognised airport was under discussion in May. Many City councillors and members of the public supported the plan wholeheartedly, believing air transport of both people and goods was going to develop. Mr H. E. Witard, the Deputy Lord Mayor, said Norwich should get a move on; in his opinion, the Council should get hold of an airport and obtain the right to establish a municipal aerodrome.

June

HRH Prince George flew to Mousehold Aerodrome in July. Unhappily his reception was marred by an accident to one of the Moth aeroplanes of his escort. The machine crashed near Mousehold Barracks, but fortunately there were no casualties. The Prince was in Norfolk to visit the Scout Jamboree at Salhouse.

July

Miss Ella Shields made her first appearance in Norwich at the Hippodrome, St Giles, during July. She was supported by a splendid variety company. Her deep, rich voice was heard each night, singing 'Burlington Bertie' and 'Smile, Smile, Smile'. Her impressions of 'Susie' by an Englishman, a Frenchman and an American were always enjoyed.

The Third Annual Flying Pageant was held in July at Mousehold and one of the attractions was formation flying by members of the Royal Air Force 19th Fighters' Squadron. Visitors, including Flight Lieutenant R. L. R. Atcherley of Schneider Cup fame, inspected an Imperial Airways Liner.

August

Prince George paid another visit to Norwich in August. He made a surprise landing at Mousehold Aerodrome, left by car for Ranworth where he had a pleasant day's duck shooting and motored back to London the same night.

October

On 21 October many Norwich people took the train to Great Yarmouth to see HRH the Prince of Wales open the new Haven Bridge, which linked Great Yarmouth with Gorleston. His Highness also inspected the fishing fleet.

Regular outings were made by Norwich people in the 1930s to see the Scottish fishing girls at Yarmouth. The fishing fleet, which reaped a harvest of herring and moored along the wharves between Great Yarmouth and Gorleston, had been part of the autumn life of Great Yarmouth for many years. In the 1880s the herring fleet employed more than 800 first class smacks of 15 tons and upwards, carrying six men each, and an even larger number of smaller vessels.

In 1930, a combined fleet of 973 craft, consisting of 767 Scots drifters and 206 Great Yarmouth craft, sailed out in search of the silver fish and landed 617,000 crans. Down from Scotland with the drifters came the Scottish lassies who gutted the herring by the wharf sides, often in biting cold winds. They filled thousands of barrels with alternate layers of salt and fish, singing as they bent over their unsavoury task.

The harbour rang to the clippety clop of heavy sea boots; the girls stood surrounded by rows and rows of wicker baskets, filled to the brim with herring. They worked so quickly and dextrously that the human eye could hardly follow their movements. At night, the Scottish girls replaced their fish-scale covered clothes for their walking-out attire, linked arm in arm, gazing at the shop windows in search of gifts to take home at the end of the season.

November

There was a good crowd at the Spring Gardens in November when the Lord Mayor opened the indoor bowls club by casting the first wood. The city's bowling enthusiasts were delighted with this additional winter activity.

When completing their new building in London Street, Messrs Jarrolds discovered an old ice well in the basement. It was 40 feet below ground level, and it was believed to have been used a century earlier for storing the ice taken from the rivers and Broads in the winter.

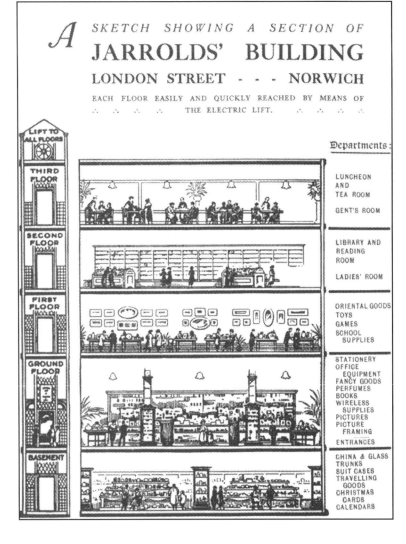

A new telephone exchange opened in Unthank Road. It was hoped that a greatly improved service would be provided, as more and more businesses and householders installed telephones.

December

By the second week of December, Christmas advertisements filled the papers. Kays Ways Pays shops at 15 Magdalen Street, 15 St Stephens and 10 St Benedict's were advertising 200 tons of peel at 6*d* a pound, mincemeat at only 5½*d* a jar, two 1-pint jellies for 3½*d* and a pound box of chocolates at 1*s* 3*d*.

Wallace Kings stores were offering a free Norfolk turkey to purchasers of their Quick Meal oil cookers, while all shoppers spending over £1 at Bretts, St Stephen's, got a handsome egg set free. Chaplin's of 37 Botolph Street were offering a free cap with every gent's or youth's overcoat.

As Christmas Day approached, a big scheme for the conversion of Thorpe Station Yard as a bus terminal, with 200 feet of covered platform, was announced.

On Christmas Eve the holiday rush to and from Thorpe Station began in mild weather. Two full excursion trains left Norwich. At Norwich stations, Post Office mail appeared heavier than usual, and the cheap fare facilities to the Midlands were well patronised.

The Theatre Royal was preparing for the twice daily showing of *Dick Whittington and his Cat*. The Hippodrome was showing John Barrymore in his first talking film, *General Crack*. On Christmas Day people forgot the trade slump and, if they could not afford to take the children to the Theatre Royal, at least there was a pantomime on the wireless. The hoped-for revival of trade and reduction in unemployment had not materialised by the year's end. Many Norwich men and women were still unemployed, but better times in 1931 were anticipated.

1931

In the first week of January there was a Variety Show on at the Hippodrome: a United Artists all-dialogue picture, *One Night of Love,* starring Lilian Gish. The Hippodrome had begun its life as the Grand Opera House, opening on 3 August 1903 with *Country Girl*.

In 1904 Bostock and Fitt took over the Grand Opera House and re-named it the Hippodrome. In 1912 there was a break in the showing of variety acts, when they showed pictures for six weeks. Moving pictures were also shown in the summer of 1909 and 1910, with two variety acts

each week. Marie Lloyd had performed there on five occasions between 1907 and 1917 singing 'A Little Bit of What You Fancy' and 'Everything in the Garden is Lovely'.

George Formby Senior had performed there in 1905, 1907 and 1909, and his banjo-playing son was there in 1925.

Sid Field came to the Hippodrome in 1926 in a revue called *Are You Listening?* Will Hay made one appearance in 1921. Now, in these difficult times for theatres, talking pictures were again being shown in this auditorium, with its four private boxes in French renaissance style and its circle stalls where cupids supported electric lamps. Surmounting the proscenium were the City Arms. On each side were full-size reclining figures representing music or poetry, and above the Coat of Arms was a handsome painting illustrative of the Arts. All this, under the main dome 25 feet in diameter, with a display balcony with overhanging flowers and from which hung a cluster of electric lights, looked strangely out of place at the talking picture shows.

There was concern in the city about the menace of continental competition to the local boot and shoe trade, mainly from Czechoslovakia. The output in

Norwich Hippodrome started life as a Grand Opera House.

Great Britain per operative per week was approximately 21 pairs; in the USA it was 30 pairs and in Czechoslovakia 114 pairs.

February

The Norwich Parks and Gardens Committee were considerably perturbed by consistent damage to trees in the city. In the previous year, 200 were destroyed.

There were few towns in England with so many trees in the streets: Norwich had between five and six thousand trees.

The Committee offered a £5 reward to anyone who could provide information leading to a conviction of people responsible for the damage.

A house once known as the Hermitage, at the junction of School Lane and Sprowston Road, was opened in February as a licensed house to be known as the Brickmakers, the old Brickmakers being a hundred yards from the new premises. The transformation of the Hermitage had been carried out by the new owners, Steward and Patteson Ltd.

Jack Dain was a long-serving and much respected Chief Constable of Norwich.

March

Amy Johnson flew into Norwich on 17 March. When asked what future she thought Norwich had as a municipal airport, Miss Johnson replied that she was convinced that within a few years all sorts of air lines would be operating in England, and she thought Norwich would have an opportunity to share in the traffic.

Miss Johnson was wearing a Norwich Aero Club badge on her coat as she climbed into the cockpit of her little aeroplane.

At this time, Woolworth's were advertising their café as having good food at the right price with good service, and nothing over 6*d*.

The Chief Constable's report in 1931 stated that the present strength of the police force was 139, excluding one policewoman who was attached to the detective department.

It had been found necessary over the year to hold only nine Juvenile Courts: the number of young people brought before the courts during the last few years had been very small, because the circumstances had allowed a caution to be administered to the offenders.

Police officers mounted on motor cycle combinations had been patrolling the city, and now the Council were being asked to sanction the purchase of three BSA tri-cars for these motor patrols.

There had been 17 fatal accidents in Norwich during 1930, and 68 children had been found wandering in the streets, and 27 animals found straying. Some 311 cautionary notices had been issued to traders in respect of defective weighing instruments.

As river traffic had increased, a motorboat was purchased for patrol work on the river. The jurisdiction of Norwich police extended to Hardley Cross at the junction of the rivers Yare and Chet.

April

This month saw remarkable developments on the country side of Mile Cross, beyond Boundary Road. Houses and bungalows were for sale: three-bedroom semi-detached bungalows were priced at £550, with a deposit of £25. Three-bedroom houses were priced at £575. These were being built by Bush Builders Ltd of Aylsham Road and 14 Bank Plain.

May

There was a sudden reduction in the Bank Rate, which came down to 2½ per cent – the lowest level since 1909. The effect on trade was not thought likely to be immediate, but the reduction was a good omen.

June

Throughout June, earthquake tremors were felt throughout East Anglia. Norwich was woken on the morning of Sunday 7 June by a deep rumbling; windows rattled and ornaments shook for 30 seconds.

A new bridge was being built across the River Wensum at Guardian Road. Once complete it would form part of the Norwich Ring Road.

July

The Norwich Hospital week-long carnival began on 8 July. Some of the items planned were a pageant, dances, swimming gala, torch light tattoo, tennis tournament, bowls tournament, garden fete and displays of all sorts.

In 1930 the Norfolk and Norwich Hospital had cared for 5,973 in-patients and treated 18,025 new patients. Its income had been £48,800, expenditure £54,244.

September

It was feared that the £423,000 plan for St Stephen's Street would have to be deferred in view of urgent demands for economy in public expenditure.

A new organ, the first of its kind, was installed at the Haymarket cinema during September. Also this month, there was an impressive spectacle when Norwich Castle was floodlit.

The city's political machinery was oiled and swung into action when the Prime Minister announced the dissolution of Parliament. At the last election the results had been:

G. H. Shakespeare (Lib)	33,974
W. R. Smith (Lab)	33,690
Dorothea Jewson (Lab)	37,040
Capt. J. G. Fairfax (Con)	30,793

In the week the election was announced several hundred men and a few women marched through the streets of Norwich, a Red Banner car-

A traditional ward at the Norfolk & Norwich Hospital

ried at their head, singing the Red Flag. This was a demonstration by unemployed people against a reduction in the dole and other cuts imposed by government; a strong guard of police accompanied the marchers.

At the end of the month, long before the polling booths closed in many constituencies, a great crowd starting assembling in the Market Place to watch the results flash up on the screen displayed by Jarrold's.

Looking down from Jarrolds, a remarkable scene presented itself; thousands of people were wedged between the market stalls, and as far as the eye could see up Guildhall Hill was a sea of faces. The city police had great difficulty in keeping the Walk sufficiently clear to allow the passage of late trams.

A large proportion of the people stayed until after midnight, cheering the victories of the national government. The anticipated socialist triumphs did not materialise. As the results came in from around the country, Labour suffered unprecedented, colossal losses. In Norwich, although Mr Shakespeare headed the poll again, Mr Hartland won a Conservative seat for Norwich.

November

By November, and coinciding with early signs of an industrial revival, strong efforts were being made to attract new industry to Norwich. Many enquiries about setting up factories in the city were received from abroad.

For six days in November, the Regent Picture House in Prince of Wales Road showed Charlie Chaplin in *City Lights*, while at the Hippodrome, Maurice Chevalier starred in *Playboy of Paris*, with Clara Bow in *No Limit* taking second place on the bill.

Norwich was declared Bus Centre of East Anglia in November. From their new offices in Thorpe Road a huge network of Eastern Counties services covered the whole of Norfolk, Suffolk and Cambridgeshire, and parts of Northamptonshire and Huntingdonshire.

December

It was hoped that this month would see another step being taken in the establishment of Norwich Municipal Aerodrome: an official enquiry into the question was to be held at the Guildhall, under the Air Navigation Act 1926.

The City Council had applied to the Minister of Health for authority to borrow £24,468 to level the land at Mousehold.

As the Christmas shopping rush began in Norwich stores, the slogan was 'Buy British'. Although no more business had been done than in the previous year, the pound had never before offered such good value.

This point was well illustrated in a local paper which gave as an example a typical family of four: mother, father and two children, given a pound to spend on Christmas presents. Mother could have a leather handbag with zip fastener for five shillings and sixpence; father could be given a London-made briar pipe for three shillings and sixpence. For five shillings the daughter could be given a paint box while son could be bought a model aeroplane that could fly a hundred yards, for six shillings.

Milder weather was forecast for Christmas 1931. There was a shortage of turkeys, the price being 2s 2d a pound for Norfolk birds. Meanwhile, the trade depression was forgotten as braziers glowed on the Market Place and flickering paraffin lamps illuminated the stalls. In the shops there was a brisk trade in wireless sets and gramophones; all over the city wireless poles were being erected hastily.

1932

With the coming of the New Year, the *Eastern Evening News* celebrated its Jubilee; the newspaper had been founded on 2 January 1882.

On 4 January the paper reported a striking improvement in East Anglia's railway services when, during a trial run between Thorpe and Liverpool Street Station, the LNER engine *Sandringham* reached speeds of ninety miles an hour, and the excursion train completed the journey in just two hours and six minutes.

February

The Carlton Cinema in All Saints' Green opened. The new theatre could accommodate 1,000 people in comfort. Musical interludes were provided by a well known London musician and his orchestra.

During this month, the Norwich shoe factory of Messrs Barfield and Richardson was reduced to a charred ruin. Flames leapt 30 feet above the roof of the factory in Botolph Street; two fire engines attended the scene, one stationed in Botolph Street and the other in Magdalen Street, but they could do little to save the building.

The month also saw a gold rush in Norwich and Norfolk, as people turned out their hoards of sovereigns, jewellery and trinkets. Mr Bloomfield, the jeweller of Bank Plain, said he had been buying sovereigns over the previous three months at an average rate of 10,000 a week, but on 24 February people were queuing up and he was buying 1,000 an hour. He was paying 27 shillings for each coin. Correspondingly high figures were being paid for gold jewellery.

March

When the Kennel Club admitted the registration of the Norwich Terrier in March, people wondered whether it would rise to fame like the Norwich Canary. The origin of the breed was something of a mystery: a Mr Nichols of Wymondham bred a small red dog in 1880 which he called a Norwich Terrier. They were also bred by Mr R. J. Read in 1909. When they were recognised by the Kennel Club, a Norwich Terrier Club was formed to help the breed become successful.

The new Norwich Speedway and Sports Stadium at Aylsham Road opened on Easter Sunday. It was one of the fastest tracks in England. Four thousand tons of soil had been used to make the track, which had then been dressed with gravel and cinders. A grandstand which would give covered seating accommodation to between 1,500 and 2,000 spectators was in the course of construction.

On 29 March Revd H. F. Davidson, Rector of Stiffkey, appeared before the Norwich Consistory Court sitting at Church House, Westminster, to answer charges against his moral character. The charges had been brought by the Bishop of Norwich and were:

1. Immoral conduct from September 1921 until November 1932 with a named woman.
2. In or about the month of August 1929 he was guilty of immoral conduct in that he annoyed and made improper suggestions to a waitress at a café in Walbrook, London.
3. On 12 November 1931 he was guilty of an immoral act in that he embraced a young woman in a public room at a Chinese Restaurant in Bloomsbury.

4. During the last five years he had been guilty of an immoral habit in that he habitually associated himself with women of loose character for immoral purposes.

This case was to fill the newspaper headlines for days to come. On the eighth day of the trial a sensation was caused when Mr Davidson's solicitor announced he was withdrawing from the case because, in view of the limited funds available, the money for the defence was exhausted. On the ninth day, the Rector declined the Bishop's offer to pay part of the expenses. He did not, he said, want to be under any obligation to the Bishop. A long adjournment was granted to help Davidson raise funds to continue his defence.

April

The city's Medical Officer of Health issued a serious warning as to the dangers to which Norwich was exposed by an outbreak of a mild form of smallpox. Several cases of alastrim, the mild form, had occurred in the city in the preceding few weeks, and more cases were thought likely to occur.

On the ninth of the month the Eastern Evening News reported that a mad bull, with head down and tail lashing, had paraded the streets of Norwich for over an hour, chasing anyone who came its way. The bull had broken away from the pens at Messrs Ireland's cattle sale, Castle Meadow. It was eventually captured when it was driven into Spelman's sale yard and roped.

Armies of children besieged the Regent Theatre, Prince of Wales Road, when they opened for Saturday morning matinee shows for an entrance fee of three pence.

The Yare Rowing Club held a dinner at the Thatched Restaurant, Norwich in April to celebrate the 21st anniversary of the club.

May

Prince George flew into Mousehold Aerodrome in May to attend the consecration ceremony of the war memorial chapel at the East end of the Cathedral. He was also to unveil the Book of Remembrance.

At a special meeting at the Castle Museum in May, the City Council were asked to give their sanction to proceeding with the scheme to build new municipal offices. This meeting was to change the architectural composition of the heart of the city for the future.

On 19 May the hearing against Mr Davidson resumed at Church House, Westminster. Norwich people queued each day to buy copies of the *Evening News* in order to follow the progress of the trial. On the eleventh day, leading Counsel for Mr Davidson made a speech lasting for eight and a half hours. On the twenty-third day, the Reverend gentleman denied the charges brought by the Bishop of Norwich.

June

On Sunday 12 June Mr Davidson made an unexpected appearance at his church in Stiffkey. As he walked towards the door, a man barred his way, saying that the Archdeacon had made arrangements for the service to be taken by another preacher. However, the Rector side-stepped the man and, after a discussion with the substitute clergyman, he led the service for the 50–60 people in the church, only six of whom were parishioners.

Later that evening the church green resembled a car park, with hundreds of people lining the paths to the church. The church bell tolled for the evening service and the 100 people packed in the church waited expectantly for the service to begin at 6.30 p.m. A car containing Davidson and a lady friend drew up; he walked humbly to the vestry, which was securely locked; the Parish Clerk was approached, and the vestry door unlocked.

During the singing of the Psalms, Mr Davidson grasped the Bible from the hands of the clergyman who was reading the prayers; the latter mopped his brow, then stood aside as the Rector read the second lesson. This extraordinary ecclesiastical scandal delighted the local people.

A few days later, the Rector told reporters that he had received many requests to give humorous sketches and recitals; he had declined the invitations. He had also been offered a lecture tour in America. He said he was unable to settle his personal bills, and it was useless to wait for the outcome of the trial, since he would first die of starvation.

On 15 June the Royal Norfolk Show opened at Crown Point, Whitlingham. Despite the depression, the show was better than ever; Norfolk farmers triumphed over the county's difficulties.

The beautiful strip of parkland loaned for the show by the Lord Lieutenant of Norfolk, Mr Colman, was ideal for the show, being so close to the city.

Plans for a £25,000 sports stadium and greyhound-racing track at Hellesdon were submitted to St Faiths Rural District Council. It was to be erected on a 15-acre site with a 400-foot frontage on to Boundary Road and would be known as Boundary Park Stadium.

In the first week of the month, the Health Committee reported the proposed clearance of Distillery Yard, Saw Mill Yard and Dial Yard, Oak Street, and Chequers Yard and Waggon and Horse Yard, Coslany Street. The dwelling houses in these yards were unfit for human habitation because of sanitary defects and disrepair.

July

The first organised boat race within the city boundary for many years took place on 14 July. The course was from the railway bridge at the Norwich end of the new cut to Pulls Ferry: the race was against time and nine boats competed.

The newspapers reported the eagerly awaited result of the case against Revd H. F. Davidson on 8 July. The Norwich Consistory Court at Church House, Westminster had found Davidson guilty of immoral conduct. He was found guilty of molesting and importuning young waitresses in a restaurant and guilty of immoral conduct with two women – Rose Ellis and Barbara Harris. Sentence was deferred in view of a possible appeal.

On 16 July it was reported that the suggested figure for the purchase by Norwich Council of the Norwich Electric Tramways Company was £175,000. This figure included the bus service, and it was hoped that bus services would gradually replace the trams.

On 13 July Harold Davidson was refused leave to appeal against his conviction, and on 10 August the Bishop signed a notice inhibiting him on the expiration of a 14-day period.

September

Although many hoped that the Davidson affair was now closed, this was not to be. In September a crowd of 400 people assembled outside Blackpool police station, where Mr Davidson was answering a summons. This followed his appearance in a barrel on Central Beach, Blackpool, where a crowd estimated at 1,200–1,400 people obstructed the highway.

October

Queen Mary had a great reception when she came to Norwich on 15 October. In the afternoon Her Majesty opened the new Nurses' Home at the Norfolk and Norwich Hospital.

On the following day, the Bishop of Norwich dedicated the new Church of St Anne at Earlham.

Feelings ran high at a meeting of Norwich City Council on 18 October, following criticism of the delay in informing the Council of the Ministry of Health's refusal to sanction a loan for the proposed new Town Hall.

Later in the month, at a special sitting of the Consistory Court at the High Altar of Norwich Cathedral, Harold Davidson was deprived of his living as Rector of Stiffkey and Morston, and removed, deposed and degraded from the office of Priest and Deacon. At last the case gradually ceased to be the main topic of conversation.

A statement was issued by the Ministry of Health on 25 October confirming that the loan for building the new council offices had not been approved. A desperately disappointed City Council asked whether the Ministry would be willing to consider proposals for continuing with just part of the scheme. The Minister agreed to consider the suggestion, and said that, in any event, he would sanction a loan for the separate and smaller scheme to build a fire station.

At least Boundary Park Greyhound Stadium was planning an official opening on Saturday 15 October, despite earlier setbacks. Norwich would have a first class greyhound-racing track. Many Norwich firms had played a part in its construction: Yaxleys of St Giles had supplied the steelwork and Barnards Ltd and Edward and Edward had contributed to the building.

Harold Davidson and barrels

November

As unemployment increased in the county, the unemployed workers' movement joined their fellow workers to march on a hunger strike through London. A contingent from Norwich was present. They came back from London on 5 November wearing heavy packs and carrying sticks. Before returning to their headquarters in Ber Street they held a meeting on St Catherine's Plain. They carried two red banners depicting a model of the Norwich Canary perched above the hammer and sickle.

At Norwich Castle Museum, world turmoil was forgotten as the Norfolk and Norwich Art Circle's Annual Exhibition was opened by its President, A. J. Munnings.

In November, radio was the entertainment of the age; all leading wireless shops in Norwich were advertising their latest models. For example, a Philco could be bought for 16 guineas and paid for by putting £3 down and then paying 12 monthly payments of twenty-four shillings.

Willmotts of Prince of Wales Road advertised Portable 6-valve wireless at £17 17s 0d; 4-valve radiograph at £29 8s 0d and Auto Radiograph de luxe at £94 10s 0d. Messrs Rank & Son Ltd, 29 St Giles Street, had Columbia Auto Radiograph de luxe at 90 guineas, while Messrs L. E. Dunham, of 165 Aylsham Road, had Supernet Seven at 24 guineas.

December

As Christmas approached, many records were being sold as Christmas presents. The famous Columbia, on their Parade series, had a brilliant gathering of stars. Their crazy pantomime records topped the bill with such notables as Flanagan and Allen, Norman Long and Binnie Hale. On one record, Harry Tate played the Fairy Queen.

There was some good news for Christmas: for the first time, licensed victuallers were allowed to keep their houses open until 11 p.m. on Christmas Eve and Boxing Night.

The tram centre at the bottom of Rampant Horse Street in 1935

On Boxing Day a new suburban cinema, called the Capitol, opened at Aylsham Road. On the first night, the film shown was *Tarzan the Ape Man*, starring Johnny Weismuller and Maureen O'Suliivan. Ticket prices were 1s 6d, 1s 3d, 1s and 7d, and there was a free car and cycle park adjoining the cinema.

There was plenty of entertainment over the Christmas period. At the Haymarket Cinema, Laurence Olivier and Zasu Pitts starred in *Westward Passage* while at the Regent *Dancers in the Dark* starred Jack Oakie, Miriam Hopkins and George Raft. If comedy was preferred, Sandy Powell and Alf Gaddard were appearing in a film at the Carlton called *The Third String*. The Spring Gardens hosted a grand Christmas Programme and Carnival Dance.

1933

New Year heralded the shop sales. Buntings of St Stephen's and Rampant Horse Street were to the fore with underwear bargains: woven combinations at 1s 9d; nightdresses at 2s; knickers, 2s 9d, and all wool cashmere knickers with full elastic at knee and waist in fawn, cloister grey or navy were 2s.

There were hundreds of pounds' worth of household goods on sale at Garland's and many more bargains to be had at Boston's in Orford Hill, Jays in St Stephen's Street, Jarrold's in Exchange Street and Messrs Moon's, Mace's and Jarvis of St Benedict's, who all filled their windows with cut price goods.

Because of opposition to the purchase of Norwich Electric Tramways, the people of Norwich were asked to give their opinion at the polls. The opposition put forward their position on loudspeakers mounted on a motor van. Some 62,950 citizens were entitled to vote at 44 polling stations.

Only 29% of the people voted, and the proposition was rejected, with the result being:

Against purchase:	*11,033*
For purchase:	*7,775*

By the end of the month, the weather had reached arctic levels in Europe. In Norwich a temperature as low as 20.2°F was recorded. One person who welcomed the weather was the seller of hot chestnuts and drinks, who pushed his wares along the Walk in a handcart. People crowded round the cart to warm themselves while they waited for their hot nuts and baked potatoes.

By the end of the month, as they were eating their purchases, their attention was caught by the husky voice of the newspaper seller shouting his headlines: 'Hitler appointed Chancellor'. Adolf Hitler's fascist demands included having his Nazi followers appointed to most of the important ministries and official recognition of his storm troopers. People read the headlines, but were not really interested; Germany was a long way away, and did not really concern them.

March

A priceless link with the Norwich of Old Crome, the mill on Mousehold Heath, was destroyed by fire on 23 March. Only a heap of blackened bricks and charred woodwork was left of a Norwich landmark which had once been a graceful building.

April

The boot and shoe industry experienced an improvement in trade during April. More workers were taken on and many factories worked at full

Norwich shoe styles in an illustration of the early 1930s

pressure on Good Friday in order to cope with orders. The streets of Norwich once again echoed to the clatter of powerful presses and the hum of machinery.

The Mitre public house, a modern licensed house built by Bullard & Sons, was opened in Earlham Road in April. At the back of the bowling green, an up-to-date pavilion and billiard room had been built for the benefit of the Mitre Bowling Club.

The Lord Mayor, Mr H. M. Holmes, opened the latest addition to the array of public parks in Norwich, Waterloo Park. Work on the park had begun two years previously as an unemployment scheme and the work was completed on 25 February. The project had employed 65 men for 117 weeks at a cost of £37,000.

Waterloo Park remains a pleasant and major facility for the citizens of Norwich.

May

By May, the shoe factories were booming; one factory had to turn down an order for 20,000 pairs of shoes because it simply was not possible to fulfil the order by the required date. There was a shortage of female labour in the factories.

The drab colours of the last two or three years had given way to a variety of colours for the new season.

The bowling season started in May. Woods were being polished at Carrow Jubilee Club, who were having to get used to the novelty of being in the second division of the NBA, having been relegated from the first division at the end of the last season.

Settlement House were another club hopeful of regaining their place in the first division, which they had also forfeited the previous year. The Gladstone Club were opening on a new green. Members had been perturbed when they discovered that the fire station plans could necessitate the loss of a site which had been sacred to them. Over the preceding few years there had been a great improvement in the standard of many of the greens, and the Gas Works, LNER and Wincarnis Clubs were all proud of their newly laid greens.

Showery weather was not allowed to interfere with the traditional May Day celebration by the Labour Party in Norwich on 7 May. A lengthy procession formed on the Cattle Market, behind the Castle, headed by the British Legion Band and the Norwich Imperial Band. They marched through the city to the Market Place, where a large crowd waited. Among the banners carried were those of the Norwich Trades and Labour Council, the Norwich Union of Boot and Shoe Operatives, the National Union of Railwaymen and the Norwich Labour Women. The procession was also joined by the ILP, a communist section.

One of the resolutions enthusiastically carried was that 'We view with the utmost detestation the increasing evidence of the growth of Fascism, Militarism and Imperialism, which has manifested itself in political unsettlement, economic rivalry, trade embargoes, military aggression and threats of war'.

June

The Prince of Wales opened the Norwich Municipal Airport at Mousehold on 21 June. After inspecting the airport's new clubhouse, His Royal Highness took off for King's Lynn to attend the Royal Show.

July

The famous variety star Miss Nellie Wallace appeared at the Theatre Royal on 17 July; the show had come direct from London and was much appreciated by Norwich audiences.

The headlines of the Eastern Evening News *on 24 July reported that Jim and Amy (Johnson) Mollison were lying in hospital after their all-black transatlantic plane Seafarer had crashed in a field in Connecticut, USA. Within sight of the lights of New York, where thousands of people had gathered to welcome them, the Mollison plane had run out of petrol and crashed. Even so, a number of records had been broken:*

- *Amy Mollison was the first woman to fly the Atlantic from east to west.*
- *They were the first man and wife team to fly the Atlantic together.*
- *Jim was the first airman to conquer twice the east to west crossing.*
- *It was the first non-stop flight from England to the United States.*

In their Annual Report, Norwich City Football Club recorded a loss on the last season of £900 2s 11d. Increased wages and additional expenditure on improvement of the ground to provide more accommodation were thought to be responsible for the loss. The Club's annual reserve account showed that receipts from Football League games at the Nest were £13,226, compared with £12,506 in the previous year.

There was a busy day this month at the Shire Hall Police Court. A 20-year-old youth was sentenced to 21 days' imprisonment with hard labour for stealing a pair of rubber boots; a labourer was summonsed for driving a motorcycle without two independent brakes in working order and was fined 10 shillings, with 1s 4d costs, and a butcher was fined 10s 0d for failing to keep a record of the movement of five pigs at Harford.

Spectators lined both banks of the Yare at Whitlingham Reach for the Norwich Regatta on 22 July. There were 27 events on land and water, including life saving demonstrations and water polo. As usual, Whitlingham Gardens were put at the disposal of the Regatta by Mr Russell Colman, Lord Lieutenant of Norwich. One feature greatly appreciated was the swimming display by the Norwich Swan Swimming Club.

The end of month gave Norwich its third heat wave of the year. On 26 July a temperature of 82.9° in the shade was recorded. July had started with an eight-day spell of sunshine; for ten consecutive days the temperature had been above 70°.

August

By August, a record rush to the coast was under way. At Thorpe station, trains with ten or a dozen carriages were leaving every 20 minutes, from 7 o'clock in the morning. Queues of people six or seven deep waited to board the trains. Prince of Wales Road was crowded as young flappers in beach pyjamas and older men in bowler hats and brown shoes rubbed shoulders with youths in bright yellow shirts and lizard skin shoes. Doctors had been preaching the benefits of solar rays so girls had shed their stockings and wore sleeveless dresses; a few even favoured hikers' shorts. Special trains were put on in the evening; for a return fare of one shilling, trippers could travel third class on the 6.49 and return on the 10.50 from Great Yarmouth, arriving back at 11.25.

At a weekly meeting of the Norwich Rotary Club, a speaker registered a strong protest against the scanty costumes worn by men and women on the Broads; the Broads were being spoilt, in his view, by the nudist mode that had come into fashion there.

Another public house opened in August to meet the growing requirements of the district of Catton. Steward and Patteson Ltd opened a convenient and up-to-date licensed house in Catton Grove called Park House.

Norwich parks resounded to music on Sundays. At Waterloo Park the Norwich Railway Military Band were performing; the Municipal Military Band played on Mousehold Heath, while the band of the British Red Cross Society entertained a large crowd at Eaton Park. The Imperial Brass Band could be heard at Chapelfield Gardens from 3.30 to 5 o'clock, where a collection was held on behalf of the Jenny Lind Hospital and the Band's funds.

October

A minor upheaval was caused to traffic in October when tram tracks were relaid at St Giles.

A new brick and tiled bungalow just three miles from Norwich was advertised for sale by means of a small deposit and then 8s 10d a week.

For people moving to the outskirts of the city, a secondhand, coach-built 1930 Austin 16 saloon car could be bought for £125; the sum of £70 would buy a 1932 Morris Minor in excellent condition.

November

In the early hours of the morning of 5 November the Spring Gardens ballroom was gutted by fire; a dance had been held there the night before.

Norwich Labour Club opened a new headquarters at Brunswick Lodge, Newmarket Road. The Party had previously put up with inadequate office accommodation at Guildhall Chambers. The new premises were both elegant and convenient. Mr F. C. Jex, the Chairman of Norwich Labour Club, presided at the opening.

The premier girls' school in Norfolk, Norwich High School, formally opened its new buildings at Eaton Grove, Newmarket Road, on 30 November. The school had been housed in the Assembly House, but this was thought to have become too small and too old fashioned. The school had grown rapidly over the previous five years, and now had 358 pupils.

December

Yet another public house, the Constitution, was opened in December by Bullard & Sons. It was located at Constitution Hill, Norwich.

A fire destroyed the shoe factory of Messrs Barker and Ramsbottom of Pitt Street just before Christmas, throwing 70 people out of work.

Mr Dain, the Chief Constable, praised the sobriety of Norwich people over the Christmas period. There was only one charge of drunkenness, and that occurred on the Saturday before the holiday had really begun, Christmas Day being the following Monday.

Norwich City Football Club had a joyful Christmas: they defeated Crystal Palace at Selhurst Park on Christmas Day and again at the Nest on Boxing Day.

1934

At the Carlton Cinema in All Saints Green, Metro-Goldwyn-Mayer films were to be the main output. This film company was reputed to be making films at the rate of one a week. Among its films chosen for Norwich during the coming year were *Gold Diggers of 1933*; *Bitter Sweet*; *The Girls from Maxims*; *Sorrel and Son*, and *Reunion in Vienna*.

Jack Forster, the holder of the Eastern Counties Welter and Middleweight titles, attracted a big crowd at the Corn Hall, Exchange Street, in the first week of the year.

Ginger Sadd, who was also on the bill, displayed good ring judgement but was defeated by Fred Dyer who, two years previously, had out-boxed Jack Forster.

Rebecca, the Greek-style statue in Chapelfield Gardens, reappeared after spending some time in a shed during alterations to the layout of the gardens.

Slum clearance in the city was carried a stage further in the second week of the month when the Health Committee authorised two schemes: one at the back of City Road, involving 13 houses, and the other at Cowgate and Barrack Street involving 130 houses. Some 445 people were rehoused.

In the Cowgate area, 14 shops and business premises were affected; the area covered by the scheme was near Bull Close and involved Pipe Burners Yard and Wood Entry Yard.

February

In the first week of February the well-known blind organist Mr Eddie Gates was performing at the Carlton, playing his Compton organ.

The beginning of the month saw the opening of an amazing new project in a building which had formerly been a stable and a woodshed. A 13-year-old Norwich boy began business as a cinematograph proprietor. The boy, Alfred Warminger, had opened his theatre at the rear of his father's premises, the Globe Inn in Globe Street.

The children of South Heigham eagerly awaited opening night. It was very successful: over 150 children cheered Charlie Chaplin, Rin Tin Tin and

other films. Young Master Warminger was his own manager, operator and cashier; he had an assistant commissionaire who wore a chocolate and gold uniform. The entrance fee was one penny.

The woodshed cinema had been transformed by mural decorations, including a canvas panorama of Venice and Italian lake scenes. The cinema brought back memories of the very early days of moving pictures in Norwich, for the narrow high back seats covered in red plush had first been used in Mr Charles Thurston's show on Norwich Hill, when moving pictures were the wonder of the age. Norwich magistrates granted a music licence to Mr Arthur Warminger, licensee of the Globe Inn, on behalf of his son.

Later in the month, Norwich City Council were congratulated on their decision to provide a yacht station at Riverside Road. After years of neglect, Norwich was beginning to realise the potential value of its rivers.

On the 27th of the month, a public enquiry was held into the City Council's proposal for sanction to borrow £226,000 to build new municipal offices. The Council were asking for a 40-year loan. The Town Clerk explained that the actual sum would be £192,000 – the difference between the two figures was accounted for by six estimates for sewers, steelworks and the layout of the Market Place.

Nobody could deny that a city like Norwich desperately needed new municipal buildings; the conglomeration of rat-infested buildings that housed the city's administration was full to overflowing. The large corrugated iron hut on Market Place that was used by the police was unbelievable. Norwich, due to the decision reached, was never to look the same again.

March

There were exciting headlines in the newspapers on 3 March: HIGH EXPLOSIVE IN THE CASTLE MUSEUM. It seemed that two lumps of what appeared to be metal had fallen onto a Lowestoft trawler's deck from the trawl net. The mate made sure the find was looked after carefully, and put it by the stove in his cabin. As soon as he reached port, he posted it to the museum which identified it as 10 lb of TNT. Fortunately nobody was hurt, but the incident shook many people.

Trams mix with grand motor vehicles and humble horse and cart outside Norwich Guildhall.

Norwich Aero Club produced a leaflet advising Norwich citizens to learn how to fly. An annual subscription to the Club cost three guineas; flying kit, goggles, etc cost £1 5s 0d; eight hours' instruction was £14; three hours' solo flying cost 25 shillings an hour, then there was the RAeC examination fee (one guinea), Air Ministry licence (five shillings) and a Pilot's Log Book (two shillings). In fact, for £23 11s 0d, you could become a pilot.

After consultation with his officers, the Chief Constable reported to the Watch Committee that a 30 mph speed limit should be introduced generally throughout Norwich.

The Chief Constable objected to the renewal of licences for the Alexandra, the Bluebell (Lower Goat Lane), the Free Trade Tavern (St Peter's Street), the Guildhall Stores, the Oak Shades (Lower Goat Lane), the Red Rose (Back of the Inns), the True Comrade and the Wild Man (Bedford Street).
In a general survey of the area within a 50-yard radius of the Guildhall, there were 94 licensed premises, comprising 84 full licenses, two beer licences and eight off-licences. This was nearly a quarter of the number of licences for the whole city.
Of the Alexandra, the police said there were 17 fully licensed houses within 200 yards, and it was a very old house with a narrow dark staircase

running up from the smoke room: its sanitary accommodation was also unsatisfactory.
The licence of the Bluebell was renewed; it was one of the few Tudor buildings in the city to continue as a public house.

Five of the Norwich hunger marchers who had taken part in the recent demonstration in London gave an account of their experiences at the Keir Hardie Hall. The leader said that the Norwich contingent of 19 men was the largest, in proportion to the population of the city. Theirs was also the only contingent to walk into London at full strength. The longest distance marched in any one day had been 24 miles.

The numbers of local people unemployed in 1934 were:

	Men	Women
February 1934	5,354	513
1933	7,004	1,248
1932	5,849	937
1931	5,078	1,368
1930	3,961	771

April

The main topic of conversation in the streets of Norwich in March was football. The days of miracles were not passed, it was being said, when Norwich City Football Club beat Coventry and moved up to the Second Division.

Later in the month, the Lord Mayor, Mr F. C. Fox, had the pleasure of formally opening the new Thorpe Hamlet Senior Girls' School at Telegraph Lane.

May

Messrs Buntings, at the corner of St Stephens and Rampant Horse Street, held an exhibition of Norwich-made silks in the first week of May. They boasted that there was a Norwich-made fabric for every occasion. Beautiful fabrics filled their windows: super satin and crêpe suede at 3*s* 11½*d* a yard; and super sand crêpe at 4*s* 11*d* a yard.

Messrs Laurence Scott Electro Motors Ltd invited representatives from important electrical and industrial firms to Norwich to watch the manufacture of the first totally enclosed electric motors ever made. They were being manufactured at their Gothic Works for the Swansea Power Station.

June

The stigma of having no adequate swimming facilities was removed in June when the 'Lido' swimming pool was opened in Aylsham Road. This private enterprise project had been developed by Mr V. E. Harrison, and was greatly praised by the Lord Mayor, Mr Jex, when he opened the pool formally.

It was open seven days a week, and it was floodlit after 9.30 p.m. Entrance fees varied between 4*d* and 1*s* 6*d*, depending on times.

On the afternoon of 22 June a fire broke out at the Theatre Royal and swept rapidly through the building. It soon became apparent that the whole building was doomed. The theatre had replaced one that had been built on a nearby site by the famous Norwich architect Thomas Ivory. The existing building had been constructed in 1826 at a cost of £6,000, although considerable improvements had been made since that time. So little could be saved from the fire: all the valuable etchings showing earlier playhouses were lost. Lost too were old playbills and photographs, all of them irreplaceable.

Within a few hours of the outbreak of fire, the theatre's manager, Mr Harry Briden, was making arrangements for Alfredo's Orchestra and supporting variety company to give emergency performances that night. The Corporation allowed the theatre to use St Andrew's Hall.

One of the supporting acts with Alfredo that week was the Shamvas, a rope spinning, stock whip manipulation act. Peggy Shamvas was a Norwich girl and was staying with her family in the city. They had lost most of their beautifully embossed costumes in the fire, but had been able to save some of their equipment. Many of the performers had managed to get through windows of their dressing rooms to save their costumes. Alfredo's orchestra had saved most of their instruments in this way. In true show business style, the show went on!

Workmen who were removing a wall and working on the roadway near to the Castle entrance found 15 skulls and a complete skeleton in the wall,

Rampant Horse Street, pictured in 1936.

over a period of several days. The manner in which the remains were found supported the theory that bodies were put there during the Black Death or one of the plagues.

Another theory was that they had been put there after executions by hanging had taken place at the bottom of the Castle drive.

All the remains had been in one comparatively small section, and the skeleton lay in a way which suggested it had been dumped there without ceremony.

September

On 17 September the Lord Mayor opened the Enterprise, the new Norwich talkie cinema, owned by the 14-year-old Alfred Warminger. It was the only cinema in the county to be fitted with 16mm sound apparatus, 35mm being the usual size. Situated in Northumberland Street, the new cinema cost £1,500 to build and equip. Alfred Warminger had engaged a 16-year-old manager to run his children's silent cinema in Globe Street, while he looked after his new venture. The new cinema accommodated 350 people, and seat prices were a penny for children and three pence for adults.

Alfred Warminger advertises his cinema in the Silver Jubilee parade, 1936.

1935

There was a mixture of films showing at Norwich cinemas in the New Year: Mae West at the Regent, Prince of Wales Road; Anna Neagle in *Nell Gwynne* at the Carlton, All Saints' Green, and Edward G. Robinson in *Dark Hazard* at the Cinema in Magdalen Street. If dancing was more your style, Roy Fox and his band were making a personal appearance at the Lido Ballroom, Aylsham Road, and there was dancing at the Venetian Ballroom in St Andrew's Street.

Other entertainment on offer included Zasu Pitts in *The Meanest Gal in Town* at The Empire Theatre, Oak Street, for lovers of comedy, and there was a dinner dance at the Thatched Restaurant in the second week of January. The cost of the latter was 5s 0d for the dinner dance or 2s 6d for dancing only. Music was by Percy Cohen and his band.

Alderman Jex renamed Mile Cross School the Norman School during the month, and at the end of the month the YWCA moved home from Tudor Hall, Rose Lane, where their premises had become unsatisfactory, to the Girls' High School, Theatre Plain.

Because of growth in interest in Christian Science in Norwich, a large church was built in Recorder Road with seating for 300 people.

The police force was hoping for an increase in its strength. There were currently 145 officers, consisting of the Chief Constable, a Superintendent, a Chief Inspector, five Inspectors, 15 Sergeants and 122 Constables. There had been seven vacancies which had remained unfilled for economic reasons, but with the increase in the population in the city, the Chief Constable was asking for the force to be increased.

The Corporation had built 4,276 houses during the previous 15 years and the private sector was responsible for almost 2,000 more. The census showed an increase in the population of nearly 5,000 between 1921 and 1931.

February

Her Majesty Queen Mary visited Norwich on 2 February to lay the foundation stone of a new church, St Catherine's, at Mile Cross.

The Queen had motored from Sandringham and was received at the boundary of the city by the Lord Mayor and Lord Lieutenant of Norfolk.

A general air of expectancy hung over the city on 16 February: Norwich City Football Club and Sheffield Wednesday were playing to decide which of them was to be among the last eight clubs in the FA Cup Final. By 12 o'clock, the Nest was besieged by fans; the crowd was so great that officials decided to open the gate early. Norfolk people were bitterly disappointed when Sheffield Wednesday scored the winning goal just 16 minutes before the end of the game.

Norwich rang to the sound of pounding hammers as demolition gangs tore down houses to make way for the new municipal offices, which were finally to be constructed. Clouds of dust filled the air as Wounded Hart Lane was pounded to the ground.

Old Norwich was disappearing; history was being stamped out like a fly underfoot. It was not only the heart of the city that was going: houses in Oak Street were also being brought to the ground.

In St Giles, a fine old Georgian house standing in a courtyard and known as Low's House stood awaiting destruction, as the frontage of Bethel Street disappeared. An inquiry was held by the Ministry of Health into the future of numbers 82–128 Barrack Street. These Tudor dwelling houses and shops contained many lovely moulded beams, and people had pleaded for them to be saved from demolition. When it was stated that a reason for demolition was the fact that the houses had no damp course, great amusement was caused when it was revealed that the Deputy Medical Officer of Health lived in a house which had no damp course!

Preparations for the Silver Jubilee of Their Majesties King George V and Queen Mary were well in hand in Norwich. The Castle, the Guildhall, the two gateways at Tombland, the Cathedral Close and the water tower at Mousehold were all to be floodlit each evening as part of the celebrations.

May
On Monday 6 May the Lord Lieutenant of Norfolk (Russell J. Colman Esq. JP) reviewed the troops. In the football field behind Britannia Barracks, a crowd estimated at 15,000 surged towards the sports field to join in the Drumhead Service. At 2.45 p.m. that day, a decorated parade started from Newmarket Road; it was a mile long and included decorated vehicles, tableaux, walkers in fancy dress, decorated cycles, riders on horses, ponies and donkeys, and private cars. Cartons of chocolates and medals had been distributed to schoolchildren under the control of Norwich Education Authority.

On Wednesday 8 May extra public assistance

Preparation for the new City Hall, April 1935

of 1s 6d per adult and 9d per child was given to non-able-bodied recipients.

By the end of the month, work on rebuilding the Theatre Royal was well under way. Norwich City Football Club was also making plans for a new ground at Carrow Road. To be built on a nine-acre plot, it was proposed to make the whole construction out of steel, and it was to provide covered seating for 500 fans.

June

At a special meeting in June, Norwich City Council accepted a tender of £211,206 from Sir Lindsay Parkinson & Co Ltd to erect new municipal offices, Council chamber and police station.

July

A fleet of new 60-seater double-decker omnibuses, ordered from the Eastern Counties factory at Lowestoft, were received and were shortly to replace the trams on the Thorpe Road and Earlham Road route. Trams on Dereham Road and Earlham Road were replaced by double-decker buses on 24 July.

August

Norwich City Football Club announced that, by a triumph of teamwork from Messrs Harry Pointer, Boulton and Paul Ltd, Gill & Son, Rupert Street and Messrs W. J. F. Taylor, Vauxhall Street, their new stadium had been erected in a remarkably short period of time. The timetable of events had been:

15 May	The FA wrote to the City drawing their attention to reports they had received as to the unsuitability of the Nest for a large crowd.
18 May	The then Chairman announced that there was a grave possibility of the Nest being declared unsuitable.
28 May	The Board agreed to accept the offer of a site near Thorpe Station.
1 June	It was announced that arrangements had been made with J. & J. Colman Ltd for the Club to take over the Carrow Road ground on a 20-year lease; tenders were invited the same day.
11 June	Dumping material for the terrace construction began.
17 August	Construction of the terraces and stands completed except for the extreme end at the riverbank.
31 August	New football stadium opened.

September

The 1,000th yacht of the season put in at the Norwich Yacht Station on 16 September. The yacht, Maid of Foam, was a hired boat owned by Jack Powles of Wroxham.

Because smaller British coasters had been built, and because the river had been dredged to enable it to be navigated by ships of ten feet draught, coal, timber, grain, cement, bricks and tiles were now entering Norwich by river. During the last five years the number of ships using the Port had increased by 170 per cent.

On 30 September the largest vessel ever to reach Norwich unloaded a cargo of cement at Foundry Bridge. The vessel, the coaster Acrity, was 500 tons, 150 feet long, with a beam of 25 feet.

October

An air service linking Norwich with London, the West Country and the continent was inaugurated in October. Planes left Norwich at 11 o'clock and landed at Croydon at 12.10 p.m. One of the first people to take advantage of the flights was Mr Charles Watling. On the return journey, with the wind behind them, the journey from Croydon to Norwich took 50 minutes.

The Lord Mayor of Norwich, Mr P. W. Jewson, unlocked the front door of 104 Berners Street, Norwich in October. This was the 5,000th dwelling house built by the Corporation. The slum clearance programme was heavy: this 5,000th house meant that sufficient houses had now been built to accommodate almost one-sixth of the population.

Under the five-year programme, in 1933 2,515 houses were to be demolished; 8,099 people displaced, and 2,045 houses and flats built.

WE THINK THAT EVERYBODY IN NORWICH MUST BE SHORT-SIGHTED BECAUSE THEIR FOOTBALL CLUB NORWICH CITY PLAY ON A GROUND WHICH IS SURROUNDED BY PEOPLE LOOKING OUT OF HOUSES. THE MAN IN THE EXTREME WINDOW IS A 'SOCCER' HATER, BUT HAS TO LIVE IN NORWICH BECAUSE HE'S AN INSURANCE AGENT.

THE GROUND OF NORWICH CITY IS CALLED "THE NEST" AND IT HAS BEEN BUILT INSIDE SO MANY HOUSES THAT ALL THE INHABITANTS OF NORWICH WHO DON'T SIT IN A WINDOW THAT OVERLOOKS THE GROUND ARE CALLED OUTCASTS AND —

FIE!

— CAN ONLY TAKE OUT NATURALISATION PAPERS WHEN THEY HAVE SAVED ENOUGH MONEY TO BUY A LADDER — THAT WILL AT LEAST GIVE THEM A FLEETING GLIMPSE OF THEIR LATEST CENTRE-HALF.

IN THE CONSTRUCTION OF THEIR GROUND NORWICH CITY HAVE CONDENSED SO MUCH IN LITTLE THAT ONE OF THEIR GOAL NETS IS SHROUDING A HOUSE TO SUCH AN EXTENT THAT WHEN A BALL GOES BY THE GOALKEEPER NEVER KNOWS WHETHER TO LOOK IN THE BACK KITCHEN OR MARRY THE GIRL.

TOM WEBSTER '33

"Daily Mail" — Nov. 20 · 1933.

November

Sir Harry Lauder made a personal appearance at the Theatre Royal in November. During his visit, Sir Harry was to be seen at Willmotts Store, Prince of Wales Road, where he autographed copies of his records.

December

The last tram to be seen in Norwich ran from Orford Place, on the Newmarket Road and Cavalry Barracks route, at eleven o'clock on Tuesday night, 10 December.

For some 35 years the trams had played an important part in the daily business and social life of Norwich. A crowd of about 500 people gathered in Orford Place to see the last tram set off. When it left, the tram was packed with people inside and outside, even standing on the conductor's platform.

Among the passengers was Mr C. Watling, a former sheriff of Norwich. He said he had ridden on the first tram, and thought he would like to ride on the last one.

As Christmas approached, Sir Oswald Mosley attended a luncheon at the Royal Hotel in order to give a short summary of the fascist policy as it affected the county.

There was nothing traditional about the weather at Christmas 1935: no icicles hung from windows; southerly winds brought dull, rainy weather. Norwich shoppers filled the Market Place, returning home laden with parcels on the new omnibuses.

1936

On 18 January the *Eastern Evening News* reported worldwide concern about the health of King George V. Three days later, on 21 January, his death was announced. He had died at Sandringham, where he had spent so much of his life.

Norwich went into mourning: black boards were placed in the windows of most shops; people wore black arm bands; there was even a noticeable effect in the shoe trade, as buyers requested early delivery of orders of black shoes.

All cinemas and theatres closed, to the disappointment of many

A Tom Webster cartoon from the Daily Mail, poking fun at the Canaries' old football ground

Norwich people as it was the last week of the pantomime *Cinderella* at the Theatre Royal.

Other entertainments hit in Norwich included Gordon Harker starring in *Hyde Park Corner* at the Hippodrome; the world's greatest tenor, Richard Tauber, who was billed at the Regent cinema in *Heart's Desire*; Paul Robeson starring in *Saunders of the River* at the Electric, *Escape Me Never* and *The Fighting Pilot* at the Empire and *The Florentine Dagger* at the Theatre de Luxe, St Andrew's Street. The Haymarket had promised a mammoth production of *Dante's Inferno*, with Spencer Tracy and Clair Trevor leading a cast of 13,000. The small Enterprise Cinema in Northumberland Street had planned to show Bill Hart in *Square Deal Sanderson* and Sid Chapman in *The Submarine Pirate*, The Cinema, Magdalen Street had to cancel Valerie Robson in *Rendezvous at Midnight*, and the Astoria in Cowgate had to forgo its plans to show a favourite of the time, Tom Walls, in *A Cup of Kindness*. Mr Nugent Monck's Norwich Players were due to be performing *The Tempest* at the Maddermarket.

Also suspended were roller-skating, which was normally held every evening at the Central Hall, near the General Post Office in Prince of Wales Road. The cost of an evening's entertainment there was one shilling for gents, with free skate hire, and sixpence for ladies, with another sixpence to pay for the hire of skates. The dances at the Samson and Hercules Ballroom, Tombland would also have been suspended, as would its other attractions: as well as the usual dances on Thursday and Saturday nights, there was a cabaret. In January 'Swifty' the amazing comedy trick cyclist was appearing and Bert Galey and the resident band were in attendance. Admission price was normally 2s 6d.

On 23 January Norfolk said goodbye to King George. After a service at Sandringham Church his body was borne on a gun carriage to Wolferton Station, watched by many Norwich people who had motored to Sandringham to pay their last respects.

April

On 8 April the Norfolk and Norwich Hospital reported a record number of in-patients – 7,035, an increase of 237 over the previous year. The number of outpatients treated was 20,308 which also showed an increase over the previous year's figure of 19,052. The total nursing staff at the Norfolk and Norwich and Jenny Lind Hospitals was 233.

As Easter approached, Norwich market stallholders were well stocked, especially with colonial fruit. The imports from South Africa made a fine display, and there were some good bargains to be found:

South African grapes, from 1s a pound
Cape plums, from 6d a pound
Spanish oranges 12 for 6d
South African pears 1d to 2d each
South African pineapples, from 6d each
Australian Cox's Orange Pippins 6d per pound

There were good quality chickens on offer at 3s to 6s 6d each; the fish market also had abundant stocks: kippers at 2d to 5d a pair; bloaters at 1s to 1s 6d a dozen; crabs from 4d each; shrimps at 6d a pint, and chilled salmon at 1s 6d to 1s 8d.

Trade was brisk despite the intense cold: it was the coldest Easter for seven years and the newspapers reported that on Easter Day there were eight degrees of frost.

May

Ginger Sadd, the Norwich boxer, retained his Eastern Area Welterweight title at the Norwich Corn Hall, Exchange Street on 17 May, when he fought Seaman Jim Lawlor.

The people in Merton Road were shaken when the whole of the rear of a house disappeared into a huge hole some 25 feet deep. An elderly couple were reported missing, presumed dead. It was many days before death was confirmed and their bodies recovered from the hole. Since 1910 there had been three such startling events in this area.

Members of Norwich Council were meeting in a very depressed mood: part of the agenda of their meeting was devoted to a discussion on the protection of Norwich citizens in the event of an air attack.

July

The Annual Natural Rose Day was held during July, in aid of the Norwich Hospital appeal. Norwich was one of the few cities where a Natural Rose Day was held: ladies offered fresh rosebuds to passing crowds, and it was estimated that there were 100,000 blooms in the streets.

The 16-year-old radio and stage star Hughie Green headed the bill at the Theatre Royal.

August

A big problem faced the management of the Theatre Royal in August; how could they accommodate the huge number of people who wanted to see Gracie Fields? Wherever Gracie appeared, her vast public followed her. Never before in the history of the Theatre Royal could anyone recall such a phenomenal demand for seats. During the week of her visit, Theatre Street was crowded – not only by those waiting to enter the Theatre but by hundreds of people hoping for a glimpse of the star.

Not to be completely outdone, the Hippodrome was showing a film entitled *The Week of Grace*, starring Gracie Fields.

September

Mr H. Fish of 209 Drayton Road picked up the sound transmission from Alexandra Park television station in September. Reports from Alexandra Park were most encouraging. The BBC had estimated that reception could be picked up at 25 miles, but they had received reports of sound reception at a range of 100 miles.

The City Council agreed to have a tower erected at the St Giles end of the new City Hall, at a cost of £7,973. On 24 September the Lord Mayor, Councillor Walter A. Riley, laid inscription stones at the entrance to the Hall. One stone bore his own name and the other was inscribed with the names of the architects, Charles Holloway James and Stephen Rowland Pierce.

Messrs Youngs Crawshay & Youngs opened another new public house, the Oval in Dereham Road. The new house derived its name from the large grass oval bed in front of the building.

November

Work started this month on the remodelling of Westlegate, which involved the erection of new shops and offices and the provision of a wide road to All Saints' Green.

Westlegate in 1921, before its widening

At the end of the month, 'Pilot Radio Services' of 71 Prince of Wales Road were advertising their rental rates: a radio cost 1s 11d a week.

With the removal of tram lines and substitution of islands, the appearance of Prince of Wales Road changed completely as trees were planted along the islands.

December

The *Eastern Evening News* reported a grave crisis between King Edward and his Ministers. The Duke and Duchess of York, who had been abroad, returned to London, and on 20 December King Edward abdicated.

The Duke of York was to be the new King. Norfolk people were

Brenner's Bazaar, later Peacock's Bazaar

delighted. Prince Albert Frederick Arthur George had been born on 14 December 1895 at York Cottage, Sandringham, Norfolk.

The accession of the new King was proclaimed in Norwich Market Place by the Lord Mayor, Mr Herbert Frazer, on 14 December and at noon on that day there was a crowd of some two to three thousand people gathered in the Market Place. A dais decorated with the Union Jack had been erected in front of the Guildhall for civic dignitaries. The National Anthem was sung and a roar of cheers for the new King echoed around the streets.

As Christmas approached, the city streets filled with shoppers. Shop windows were filled with gifts; Jarrold & Sons Ltd were selling Hornby clockwork train sets at prices between 4s 11d and 63s. Electric train sets cost between 15s and 72s. Fretwork hobby sets cost from 1s 6d upwards.

The Norwich Wireless Company had a fine array of wireless receivers: the Cossor cost £5 17s 6d, and the Lissen was £9 10s 0d. Pilot Radio of Haymarket guaranteed customers their money back if they could not receive America.

J. W. Quick Edward's Wine Vaults of Castle Street were selling Black Seal Whiskey at 12s 6d a bottle; Emu Sack Sherry at 3s 3d and Old Fruity Port at 3s 10d a bottle.

Curl's in Orford Place had some good tapestry fireside chairs for 11s 6d and beautiful oak bureaux with two drawers for £2 9s 6d.

Most tobacco shops were selling Craven A cigarettes at 75 for 4s 6d. These cigarettes were contained in a novel Rocker Blotter Casket.

The King and Queen, with the young Princesses Elizabeth and Margaret, left London by train to spend a quiet family Christmas at Sandringham.

It was said that this year the best Christmas Fair for 25 years was erected at the Cattle Market. It had changed out of all recognition compared with past years: there were new ideas, electric power and loud speakers, all of which had worked marvels. You paid your two or three pennies and went on the new roundabouts or dodgems, wall of death, or chariot race. Among the many well-known showmen represented at the Fair were the Thurstons, J. Collins, Kenny Gray and Olley Gray. Parents and children flocked to the fair.

The Norwich Post Office reported a record Christmas: a total of 646,532 letters were posted in the city.

1937

By New Year's Day, the new City Hall was beginning to take shape; three storeys were already complete, but its final grandeur was hard to visualise. The shopping public stopped to stare – some stopped to comment on the cost of the massive structure!

In the second week of the year, there was another interesting spectacle in the Market Place: the Duke of Wellington was gagged, bound and uprooted from his granite pedestal, then conveyed a quarter of a mile away to his new viewpoint in Cathedral Close.

Some interesting finds were made when the statue was lifted. A small parcel wrapped in a copy of the Norwich Chronicle and Norwich Gazette of 28 October 1854 was found. It contained coins of the period and a number of interesting documents relating to the erection of the statue.

February

The Mutual Service Club in Pottergate, a new home for the Norwich Unemployed Welfare Association, was opened in February by Mr Alan R. Colman. Mr Colman commented that, in a perfect world, one would expect the opening of such a facility to come before the erection of a new City Hall, or even the provision of a golf course.

Elsa Lanchester, the wife of Charles Laughton, appeared at the Theatre Royal in the second week of February. Miss Lanchester was playing the title role in Peter Pan; the role of Wendy was taken by the 16-year-old Dinah Sheridan.

March

On 6 March Sybil Thorndyke and Lewis Casson opened at the Theatre Royal in *Six Men of Dorset*, prior to its presentation in London. The Haymarket were showing *The Great Ziegfield* during that week.

Edward G. Robinson was starring at the Regent, Prince of Wales Road, in *Bullets or Ballots*. The Carlton, All Saints' Green, were showing a comedy, *Keep Your Seats Please,* starring George Formby, while Shirley Temple was appearing in *Poor Little Rich Girl* at the Electric, Prince of Wales Road.

April

Norwich awoke on 24 April to a very unusual situation: the familiar red omnibuses had disappeared from the streets. The busmen were on strike. Two of their demands were that rates for conductors should start at a shilling an hour, going up to 1s 4d; and that driver rates should be from 1s 2d to 1s 4d. As the strike dragged on, the streets of Norwich took on a carnival atmosphere, in readiness for the coronation of King George VI and Queen Elizabeth on 12 May. To everyone's delight, the men went back to work the day before the celebrations.

May

The coronation broadcast was relayed to St Andrew's Hall and Waterloo Park where large crowds of people had gathered. The reception was good, and during intervals in the commentary, the sounds of marching troops and bands and cheering crowds helped to emphasise the historic nature of the broadcast.

The city had used red, white and blue almost solidly in its decorations.

Cattle shows forgotten, the Agricultural Hall became an enormous ballroom. Above the Walk, the square keep of the castle was floodlit, as was the Guildhall.

Coronation celebrations in the Haymarket, 9 May 1937

Seen here in a photograph of 1935, the Boar's Head stood in the way of planners who wanted to widen St Stephen's; this impasse was overcome when the building was destroyed by a German bomb.

The Arcade had shunned bunting, preferring instead to turn itself into a garden; shrubs, intertwined garlands of flowers and hanging baskets filled with flowers ran the length of the arcade.

No street, alley or avenue was left undecorated. There was a decorated procession, military bands, dancing in parks: sober old Norwich had excelled itself!

The city came back down to earth with a bump just five days later; the busmen went out on strike again, and there was a busless bank holiday.

On 21 May the population of Norwich was woken by a violent thunderstorm. The rain was the heaviest since the flood year of 1912, and in the space of just 22 hours, 1.56 inches of rain fell.

July

In the first week of the month, Miss G. V. Barnard took up her duties as new Curator of the Castle Museum.

It was announced that the Nest, home of Norwich City Football Club for 27 years from 1908 when they left Newmarket Road until their move to Carrow Road in 1935, was soon to be sold. An ice rink was planned for Norwich, and it was thought it would be built on this site.

New signs appeared in Norwich streets in connection with parking regulations. The small signs stated: 'Halt beyond this sign on this side only'.

The new extended façade to Lloyds Bank on The Walk was thought to add greatly to the dignity of the eastern side of the Market Place.

As the City Hall slowly took shape, details of a proposed new Central Public Library were announced. The Corporation applied for compulsory powers to acquire a site that fronted Bethel Street, Lady Lane and St Peter's Street.

September

Mr Ernest Bevin, General Secretary of the Transport and General Workers Union, delivered the presidential address to the annual meeting of the Trades Union Congress at Norwich on 6 September.

On 7 September the old icehouse that gave its name to Icehouse Lane, between Bracondale and Carrow Hill, was demolished. It had stood in the garden of 7 Carrow Hill and was probably built in the early part of the 19th century.

George Robey, known the world over as 'The Prime Minister of Mirth', appeared at the Theatre Royal in September. He appeared with Sir Harry Lauder, who headed the bill.

It was with pleasure that Norwich people heard that the Old Hippodrome was to be opened again; not as a picture house, but as a Music Hall. Programmes were to be devoted exclusively to variety, and Claude Dampier was to head the bill at its opening.

After months of hard work, Norwich City Council and its officers had drawn up plans for the protection of the city's inhabitants in the event of air raids. Volunteers were to be asked to man first aid posts and to act as air raid wardens. Some 2,000 volunteers were required to train in first aid, and special classes had to be arranged.

A third branch of the air service was to be fire pickets; they would consist of messengers, fire patrols and drivers of lorries, vans and cars. Training was to be arranged as soon as there were sufficient volunteers.

The Norwich Chamber of Commerce at the Carrow old laundry arranged an air raid precautions demonstration. Incendiary bombs were exploded and police stood by wearing protective clothing and gas masks. Instructions were given on how to turn a room into an air raid shelter. Over a period of three weeks, 1,500 people attended.

On a lighter note, on 17 September Hughie Green, the 17-year-old favourite of radio and stage, presented his famous gang at the Hippodrome, in *Radio Rhythm of 1937*.

October

The new Civic Chief for Norwich was announced in October: Mr Charles F. Watling, a former Sheriff, was to be the next Lord Mayor.

An old-timer was still good enough to hold her own at the top of the bill at the Hippodrome. Nellie Wallace was in complete control, and seemed untouched by the passing years.

The boxing season opened at the Corn Hall in Exchange Street, when Ginger Sadd had a clear win over Frank Jones.

Outbreaks of foot and mouth disease caused the cancellation of the Norwich Fat Cattle Show, for the first time in 60 years of history of the show.

The Council Chamber of the Guildhall was unusually crowded at the ceremony for the election of Mr Watling as Lord Mayor. This was to be the final time the ceremony would be held at the Guildhall since by the following year it was hoped that the new City Hall would be completed. All those present enjoyed the speech made by the new Lord Mayor, a Norwich businessman. Mr Watling spoke of leaving school at the age of 11; he had not acquired much education, he said, so he had been forced to use his brains! While going to work he had

attended night school, so he could say he worked after school hours, and he schooled after work hours. He was well known in the city for his cheerful outlook on life.

November

Small crowds gathered round the Coach Makers Arms in St Stephen's Road in November to watch Mr J. Moray-Smith, the sculptor and painter, making his three dimensional public house sign on the outside wall of the building. The panel he modelled so skilfully represented St Stephen's gates at the time of Charles II.

It was announced in November that one of the last bastions of horses in Norwich – the Westwick Depot of Norwich Corporation – was shortly to fall victim to the ubiquitous petrol engine. The large stables were to be pulled down and replaced by a store. At one time the Corporation had owned 40

J. Moray-Smith's inn sign for the Coach Makers Arms shows what the nearby city gates would have looked like.

horses. *The number was now down to eight, and these were shortly to leave the depot for the last time.*

1938

The first day of the year witnessed the confirmation of an outbreak of foot and mouth disease, and 24 cows and a number of pigs were slaughtered.

Both of the Norwich theatres were showing pantomimes: Robinson Crusoe was on at the Theatre Royal, and Jack and the Beanstalk at the Hippodrome. There was roller-skating at the Central Hall every evening, and the Samson and Hercules Ballroom was hosting afternoon tea dances each afternoon from 3 o'clock to 6 o'clock. Tea was one shilling, dancing sixpence extra.

One of the pair of bronze lions, by Alfred Hardiman, guarding the new City Hall

Once again, Norwich was in the grip of cup-tie fever; crowds were pouring into the city from all over East Anglia. By 2 o'clock in the afternoon, hundreds of schoolboys were lifted over the railings and allowed to sit just inside the touchline. The gate to the 1*s* 6*d* enclosure was closed long before kick-off.

Sadly, Norwich said goodbye to the Cup when Aston Villa beat them by three goals to two. For the first time in 32 years of participation in the cup, City's interest in the competition ended with the first home match.

In St Andrew's Street a large site was being cleared for the erection of a new automatic telephone exchange.

On the 27th of the month, a new boathouse for the Norwich Amateur Rowing Association was opened at the Ferry House, King Street.

There was an outstanding attraction at the Hippodrome, St Giles, on 31 January: Henry Hall and his orchestra were making a personal appearance. This was the first time Henry Hall had taken his orchestra around the principal cities of Britain. Already the tour was a success and Norwich was to be no exception.

February

The first day of February saw the announcement that the new City Hall was to be opened in October of this year. On 4 February the bronze lions which were to guard the main entrance were delivered.

The largest cinema in Norwich, the Odeon in Botolph Street, was opened by the Lord Mayor, Mr Charles Watling, on 7 February. Containing over 2,000 seats, the cinema struck a new note of luxury.

The Hippodrome at the time was starring the well-known radio, stage and film comedian, Max Miller.

Early in the month the City Council approved without discussion the £571,000 scheme for a new sewage works. The Council also agreed to develop a nursery school on the North Earlham Estate at a cost of £8,848. It was to be the first school of its kind in the city.

At the same meeting Mr Riley, Chairman of the Air Raid Precautions Committee, recommended the appointment of an Air Raid Precautions Officer for the city, at a salary not exceeding £400 per annum.

A deputation of cyclists and motor cyclists approached the City Engineer during the month to discuss the question of road surfaces in Norwich. They had prepared a list of roads which were in a dangerous condition, most of the dangers being created by wood blocks. The City Engineer, Mr Bullough, replied that wood block paving was more durable than alternative methods, although its initial cost was greater, and it had been found to be successful in London. He was asked to reconsider schemes for wood block paving on two grounds: the surfaces caused skidding, and the blocks could work loose in a very short space of time.

The deputation also raised the question of abandoned tram lines which were causing road hazards. Mr Bullough reassured the deputation that it was hoped that all of the abandoned tramlines in Norwich would be removed within 12 months.

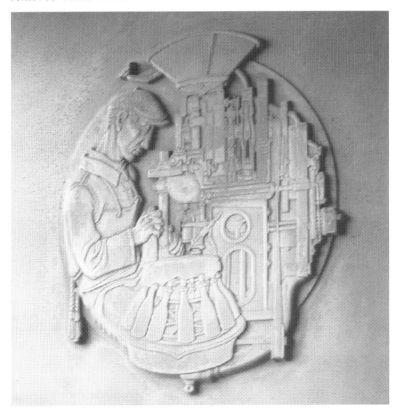

It was announced in February that Miss Kathleen Seaman, a former student of Norwich School of Art and a Norwich-born girl, was to marry Joseph Lee, the well-known cartoonist.

March

Walter Smith, a 35-year-old barge mate who had been sentenced to death at Suffolk Assizes in January, was hanged at Norwich prison in March. About 50 people gathered at the end of the private road leading to the prison, but there was no demonstration.

A £45,000 extension to the Corporation's electricity power station at Thorpe was officially opened by the Lord Mayor, Mr Watling.

By March, the new bronze doors at the main entrance to the new City Hall were in position. They contained 18 plaques by James Woodford A R A, which depicted the industries of Norwich and its historic incidents.

On 14 March another famous band leader topped the variety bill at the Hippodrome: Roy Fox, who while he was in Norwich toured many of the local shops, including Willmotts, Jarvis, Walter Littles of Magdalen Street and Mann Egerton.

Newspaper headlines on 18 March were frightening: 'Polish Troops Massing Near Border'.

Tension was brewing in yet another part of troubled Europe. Norwich shoe manufacturers, however, were more concerned about the rapid increase in the import of shoes from Czechoslovakia and Hungary during the past 12 months.

The month saw two top names in Norwich: Stanley Holloway at the Theatre Royal and Norman Long at the Hippodrome in a new version of Stanelli's Stag Party. In the first half of the programme, Shamvas and Company filled the bill with a Western novelty act. Tex Shamvas was married to a Norwich girl, Peggy Bailey, and many of her friends and relations attended the performances.

Paying the rates had an added interest in Norwich on 21 March when the

One of the panels in James Woodford's bronze doors for the new City Hall shows a worker bottling drink. Breweries and soft drinks manufacturing were major sources of employment in the city at the time.

City Treasurer's department opened for business at its new headquarters in City Hall.

After being run on the lines of a continental restaurant for 51 years, the Café Royal, London Street, entered a new phase with the retirement of Mr Stanley Erico Rayne, and the purchase of the property by Steward and Patteson. The café had been opened in 1887 by Mr Cristofero Fasola.

Opposite:
In 1938
H. Frederick Low
of the Norfolk &
Norwich Aero
Club took this
aerial photograph
of the new City
Hall. On the
left are St Peter
Mancroft church
and Sir Garnet
Wolsey pub;
on the right is
the Guildhall;
between them the
old municipal
buildings are
being demolished
and the market
itself can be
greatly enlarged to
occupy the space
thus vacated.

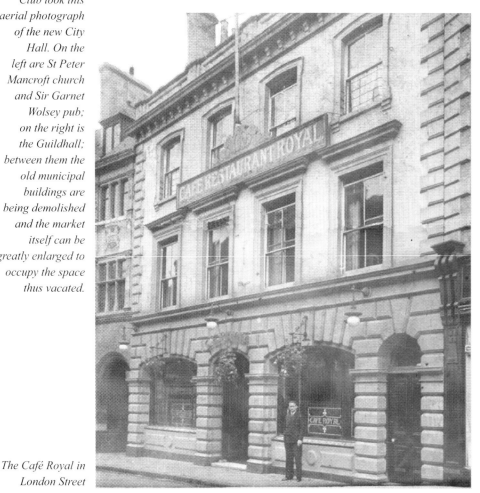

The Café Royal in
London Street

April

Another new cinema, the Regal in St Benedict's, opened its doors on 16 April. Built on modern lines, its technical equipment was of the latest type.

May

The centre of Norwich took on an unusual look on 2 May – the Market Place, around which the life of the city had revolved for centuries, was deserted. It had been cleared to make way for the demolition of the old municipal offices.

On 28 May Her Majesty the Queen drove from Sandringham to Norwich to re-open the cathedral cloister which had recently been restored, and to unveil statues of herself and the King which had been placed there.

The Norwich indoor boxing season ended on a high note on 30 May when Ginger Sadd gave a brilliant exhibition of boxing; he out-pointed George Davis and, as a result, the Eastern Area Champion placed himself in direct line for national honours. Ginger, whose real name was Arthur Sadd, had started boxing at the age of 11 and had turned professional when he was 17.

June

As the old municipal offices came crashing to the ground, the new City Hall was revealed in all its glory. It did not appear to universal acclaim: some were severely critical, and it was even described as the Norwich memorial to extravagance and mediocrity. The criticism was, though, countered by those who pointed out that the design had been selected as a result of an open competition and exhibition, when the people of the City had had every opportunity of expressing their opinion.

Norwich speedway were on an up grade: they made a fine start in the second division of the Speedway League at Sheffield.

Cotman House, the former home of John Sell Cotman who had lived and worked in Norwich from 1823 to 1833, was offered for sale by auction at the Royal Hotel. It was withdrawn at £730, and sold directly afterwards

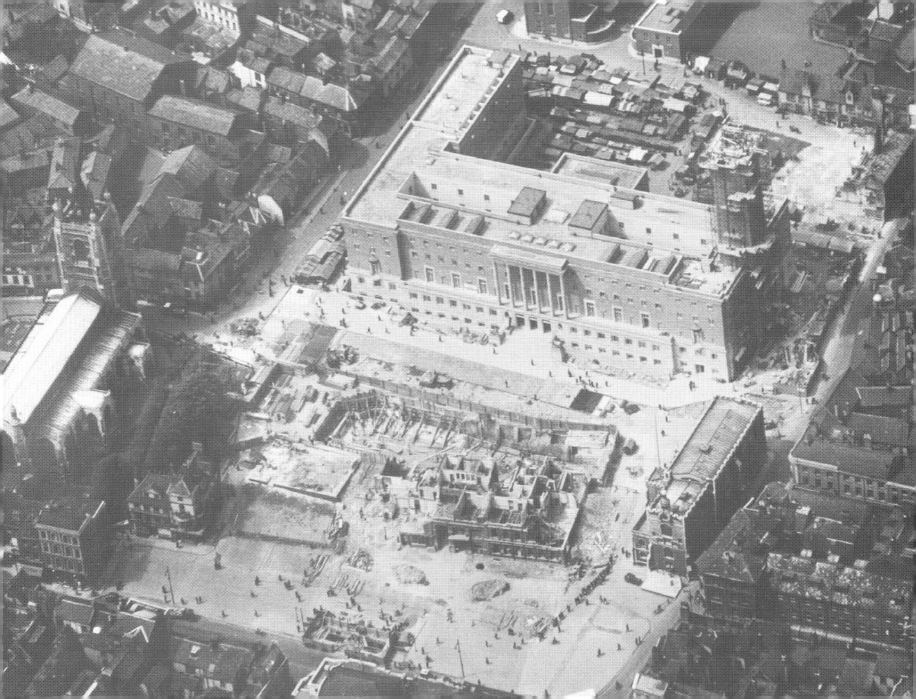

by private treaty. At the same time, the house at 7 St Martin at Palace Plain was let as flats. The house had been in the news in October 1937 when it was in danger of demolition. Strong representations from the Norfolk and Norwich Association of Architects, the Archaeological Society and the Norfolk and Norwich Arts Circle had saved the property.

With ever-increasing world tension, the City police and various Corporation departments were planning a mock blackout. All corners of street refuges had been whitewashed, and 'keep left' signs had been shrouded and fitted with low power lights. Householders were asked to make sure there was no light escaping from their windows. There were to be 100 regular police officers on duty, supplemented by 150 special constables.

After the exercise, the Deputy Chief Constable, Mr H. W. Ball, described it as a great success: Norwich had appeared to be in total darkness.

August

So popular was Shirley Temple's film *Rebecca of Sunnybrook Farm*, which was showing at the Haymarket in August, that the manager sent a telegram to Twentieth Century Fox saying: 'Shirley Temple beats the weather – house full'. The message was passed on to the young star who cabled back: 'Very pleased that Rebecca and I have beaten the weather. Love to Norwich.'

Later in the month the most talked about film *Snow White and the Seven Dwarfs* began a three-week run at the Haymarket. Apart from its humour, thrills and pathos, *Snow White* introduced several popular musical numbers. The City streets rang to the humming and whistling of 'Hi Ho' and 'Whistle While You Work'.

Some 120,000 gas masks were stored in a disused school in the city centre. The respirators were to be stored until the ARP authority's plans for gas mask stores throughout the city were finalised.

Norwich Fire Brigade gave a demonstration of their latest trailer pumps under the ARP fire-fighting scheme at the fire station.

Norwich lost an outstanding citizen with the death of Mr W. H. Scott of Laurence Scott Electromotors Ltd. He was one of the pioneers of the electrical industry and had come to Norwich in 1883, when he was little more than a youth, when Colmans had decided to take the risk of introducing electric lighting into some of their mills. He started up on his own account in a small works in King Street; the firm was called Paris & Scott.

Scott provided Norwich with its first public electricity supply from a small generating station near the fire station, with a thick overhead cable crossing St Andrew's and London Street.

September

September saw the finishing touches being made to the new Ritz cinema at the corner of Larkman Lane. The cinema had ample parking and seating for 700 people. It took 21 weeks to build, from start to completion.

At the end of the month, the issue of gas masks began in the city. About 24,000 masks were ready for distribution when the various polling stations allocated for the task of issuing them opened.

'Mr Scott in his office' – thought to be W. H. Scott, pioneer of electrical engineering in Norwich

October

On 15 October the re-erection of the war memorial in the ornamental gardens was virtually complete. The memorial had first been erected just over 11 years previously in front of the Guildhall.

Twenty of Norwich City Football Club's professional players enrolled as students at Norwich Technical College. The college Principal had approached the club with the suggestion that players should utilise some of their spare time in afternoon and evening studies, and the Club agreed to pay the fees.

On 17 October the Lord Lieutenant of the County, Mr Colman, opened the 86th exhibition of the Norfolk and Norwich Art Circle, held at the Castle. The President (Mr Geoffrey Birkbeck) and the Lord Mayor and Lady Mayoress (Mr and Mrs Charles Watling) were present.

In his opening address, the President said that little more than a fortnight previously it was thought that the exhibition was unlikely to be held, and he paid tribute to the Prime Minister for his courageous action in averting the threat of war.

On the 29th of the month, the new City Hall was formally opened by His Majesty King George VI, accompanied by Her Majesty Queen Elizabeth. The whole Market Place echoed to the cheers of the largest crowd ever gathered there as the King declared the building open, to a fanfare of trumpets.

After inspecting the new City Hall, the royal party were entertained by the Lord Mayor and Lady Mayoress to luncheon in St Andrew's Hall.

As the royal procession departed, the bells of St Peter Mancroft rang out and the immense crowd again gave the King and Queen a resounding cheer.

After lunch, His Majesty the King paid a short visit to the football match in progress at Carrow Road between Norwich City and Millwall, while the Queen went to the Norfolk and Norwich Hospital, accompanied by the Lady Mayoress, to open the Geoffrey Colman memorial.

Later in the day the King visited the Lads Club, King Street, where he was

King George VI and Queen Elizabeth opened City Hall on 17 October 1938; the queen is seen here with Lord Mayor Charles Watling and Lady Mayoress Mrs Charles Watling.

joined by the Queen. Their Majesties left Norwich for Sandringham at 3.30 p.m., leaving the Norwich people to admire their new civic building.

It had taken almost three years to build and, unlike most modern buildings, it had been constructed with solid brick walls. There were, of course, steel beams carrying the floors and spanning between the supporting walls, but there was very little vertical steelwork.

Two kinds of stone had been used to face the building: Clipstone stone from Rutland for the lowest storey and Ketton stone from Stamford for the ground floor. Above the first floor the walls were faced with handmade, multi-coloured bricks from Buckinghamshire.

The tower rose to a height of 185 feet, the four electrically controlled clock faces were 14 feet in diameter, and the bell weighed three tons.

Many beautiful woods had been used in the internal panelling; three of the five committee rooms were panelled with English ash, with inlays of Tasmanian ash, and the doors were made from oak. Sycamore framed in English oak lined the Lord Mayor's parlour, the rooms of the Town Clerk, Mr Bernard D. Storey, were in Australian walnut, while the City Treasurer's office was panelled in teak. The offices of the City Engineer and Chief Constable were lined with pressed cork tiles. Many people thought all this was altogether too grand.

Later, when the results of the municipal elections had been announced,

In front of the new City Hall are the builders' hoardings (the Garden of Remembrance not yet built); in front of those, the old-style market stalls of the 'lumber' market, on an newly extended Market Place.

members made their way to chairs of Honduran and Cuban mahogany covered in Moroccan leather. Labour had gained one extra seat from the Conservatives in the election. The constitution of the Council was now:

Labour	33
Conservatives	23
Liberals	4
Independent Labour	3
Independent	1

November

A new chapter in the history of Norwich Market Place opened this month when a man, asking for a cup of coffee at six o'clock in the morning, was the first person to be served on the new Provision Market. Since 2 May the market had been situated in Bethel Street as the original market was replaced. Now, 70 newly erected stalls covered by gaily coloured tilts were in place and within a fortnight, the Market Place was to hold 242 stalls.

Much progress in the recruitment and training of Air Raid Wardens was revealed by Mr Dain, the Chief Constable. Just over 500 Air Raid Wardens had now been enrolled, and 300 of the recruits had received training.

December

When the BBC broadcast part of the Norwich Philharmonic Society Concert from St Andrew's Hall in December, there was much satisfaction that the BBC had finally recognised the existence of the city. For years, the complaint that Norwich was almost completely ignored had been frequently expressed.

By 9 December there were still 40,000 people in Norwich who had not yet received their gas masks; there were 22,000 masks in the hands of the authorities awaiting distribution.

The unemployment figures for December were the highest since 1932. The figures, ignoring seasonal fluctuations, had remained constant for three years, but a progressive rise had begun in June 1938. In November there were a total of 6,764 people unemployed: 5,145 men and 1,619 women.

As Christmas approached, the City Engineer used 550 unemployed people to clear snow from roads and paths. The new gaily coloured awnings of stalls on the Market Place were white with snow as people thronged between the stalls to do their last-minute shopping. An uncertain year was drawing to a close.

1939

Norwich was the coldest spot in England on the night of 5 January, when 17.8°F of frost were recorded. On the Saturday of that week, frozen snow was being cleared from Norwich City's ground for their cup-tie match against Manchester City.

The weather defeated plans: heavy rain waterlogged the pitch and the match had to be postponed. Conditions were better by Thursday, but not so the fortunes of Norwich City: they were defeated 5 goals to 0 by Manchester City.

The news in January was that Norwich was not to be evacuated in the event of air raids. At this point, Norwich and Great Yarmouth were 'neutral' areas: they were designated neither to evacuate nor receive evacuees.

In the latest Ministry of Health Circular, Sir John Anderson, Lord Privy Seal and Minister for Civil Defence, was being greatly criticised about the progress of plans for air raid precautions.

In an interview he was quoted as saying: 'My opinion is that you cannot make war safe for the civilian.'

In Norwich, the first ARP badges were presented to Air Raid Wardens and Auxiliary Firemen who had successfully completed their training. In all, 243 awards were presented to Wardens, and 24 to Auxiliary Firemen.

The volunteers were fitted with gas masks before entering a specially built gas chamber at 36 Unthank Road.

Life though continued: Norwich City Council adopted a plan to build a new Technical College and School of Art on Ipswich Road at a cost of £199,000, including the cost of furniture and equipment.

Further indications of the growth of Norwich as a business centre were

displayed when a railhead store with 7,974 square feet of floor space was opened on Riverside.

The winter sale was in full swing at Moore's of St Benedict's. The bargains included:

Witney blankets, 50 x 70 inches	*4s 6d each*
Printed Jasper bedspreads	*1s 6d each*
White Turkish towels	*8d each*
White sheets, 54 x 90 inches	*2s*
Ladies' knickers, fleecy lined	*1s*
Corsets	*1s 9d each*
Brassieres	*6¾d each*
Stockings	*6d a pair*

February

The trenches dug in Chapel Field Gardens during the crisis the previous September were deepened, and flowers planted on the banks covering them.

A number of refugee children arrived during this month from Vienna, to make their homes with Norfolk families.

March

During the first week of March, the number of births registered in the city was 46; 71 deaths were registered. Seventy-five cases of infectious disease were reported during the week, including five cases of scarlet fever.

The headlines in the Eastern Evening News on 15 March read: 'German Troops March into Prague'.

St Andrew's Hall was crowded on 20 March for an Air Raid Precautions recruitment meeting; some 2,000 people were required in Norwich to fill the gap in the Civilian Defence.

Because of additional expenditure, rates were to go up by 2d, from 18s 10d to 19s in the pound.

The Chief Constable spoke of the increase in theft in the city, and the problem of young men with no interests, and nothing to do but walk the streets.

In spite of the unemployment problems, it was announced that an important development was to take place at Laurence Scott Electromotors Ltd. The company was soon to revolutionise electrical power application in the country; this was a development which promised far-reaching results and it meant the creation of a new department and the recruitment of extra staff to develop their new alternating current variable speed meter.

On the last day of the month there was a demonstration by unemployed people against the cuts in relief made by the Assistance Board.

After the demonstration, which was held outside the Agricultural Hall, a procession marched through the streets carrying a coffin bearing the inscription 'RIP killed by VAB', and a wreath with the words 'From Your Pal Ernie Brown'. The Minister of Labour, Mr Ernest Brown, was in Norwich addressing a meeting at the Agricultural Hall.

April

The well known firm of house furnishers, Robertson Colman Ltd, of 3 Queens Street, were undertaking a large rebuilding scheme. The business had been founded 100 years earlier by Henry Robertson in Howard Street, Lakenham. The business moved to Queens Street in 1884 when Thomas William Colman joined the firm.

The Theatre Royal closed in the first week of April, to open again on Easter Monday under the control of Prince Littler. His first presentation was to be Me and My Girl, the review that was breaking records in London. 'The Lambeth Walk', from the show, was being danced the world over.

A vigorous attack was mounted on the City Council at a meeting of the Norwich National Service Committee in April. It was alleged that the Council was doing nothing to help recruitment; the Market Committee had refused to allow the Territorial Army full day use of the Provision Market for a recruiting demonstration.

It was said by a Councillor that, owing to the high cost of removing the stalls, it had been decided to let them remain on the Market over the weekends in the winter months, but they would continue to be removed in the summertime.

On 20 April the Alderman Jex Senior Boys' School in Sprowston Road was opened. Mr F. C. Jex, Chairman of Norwich Education Committee, who presided over the opening, said that the school and others like it were set to give the equivalent of a secondary education to every Norwich child.

Mr George Holdinstein, of Bally Holdinstein, Norwich shoe manufacturers, said that 110 of their employees had joined the Territorial Army.

On 26 April conscription was announced. Men aged 20–21 were to be called up first.

The trenches in Chapel Field Gardens were now being made permanent by the City Engineer's Department. They were walled with reinforced concrete all round.

Proposals to utilise the chalk deposits under Norwich for deep air raid shelters were turned down on the advice of the City Engineer.

The Council was awaiting delivery of Anderson Shelters which would be distributed free to all homes where annual income did not exceed £250.

June

Elmo Stores Ltd had a grand opening in June; they boasted of their competitive prices:

Bartlett pears 7*d* a tin
Margarine 3*d*
Biscuits – 20 varieties at 4½*d* a pound
Self raising flour 4*d* per 3-lb bag

Mann Egerton of Prince of Wales Road were advertising their range of used Rover cars:

1936 Rover	£130
1934 Rover	£ 75
1938 Rover	£265

Norwich ARP services were subjected to their first test under wartime conditions in the small hours of a Friday morning; the City authorities were taking advantage of a blackout in which the whole of Norwich would be involved.

With the city in total darkness, wardens and auxiliary firemen, together with casualty, decontamination and rescue services would be summoned as an emergency. Special police would make sure all lights were out.

July

July saw the removal of the business of John Copeman & Sons Ltd from Castle Meadow and Davey Place to more extensive premises in Duke Street. Copeman's had been founded in 1789, when the firm had its premises in the neighbourhood of the Market Place.

The firm was moving to an old shoe factory in Duke Street, where extensive alterations had been needed to make it ready for Copeman's wholesale grocery and provisions business.

On 7 July the world-famous comedienne Nellie Wallace was again appearing at the Theatre Royal, heading a variety bill.

The Directors of Norwich Football Club came under criticism from one of their former fellow directors, who said that in the past four years £32,000 had been spent on transfer fees.

The Club's Chairman said that the loss on the season of £10,980 was brought about primarily by heavy expenditure on transfers but that this was justified in terms of the number of years future service the new players would give to the Club.

August

The tension caused by the threat of war, which had been gradually building, was released in a massive burst of holiday spirit on August Bank Holiday. Norwich people in their thousands flocked to the sea and countryside, travelling by train, bus and car.

The Yarmouth Road was crowded with a continuous stream of traffic. A popular holiday outfit for young girls was navy blue trousers and coloured blouses.

Prince of Wales Road was thronged with people on their way to catch trains. At Yarmouth the sea front was packed, with people walking shoulder to shoulder. One train of ten coaches contained 600 people when it arrived at Cromer's Beach Station, and it was the same story all along the coast.

The population of Cromer was thought to have trebled, and Lowestoft's beaches were crowded. The bus station was overflowing with people wanting to visit the Broadland resorts.

Holiday spirits were brought back to earth with a bump on 16 August, when 300 Anderson shelters arrived in Norwich by rail. Each shelter comprised 21 pieces, including a bag of nuts.

The delivery men did not always have an easy time: at one house a woman refused to take delivery because her husband was out, and a 70-year-old man refused to have his garden disturbed by such a thing at his age.

Demonstrations of how to erect the shelters were held at the back of City Hall. People were a little disheartened when it took three Norwich Corporation labourers nearly five hours to erect just one shelter!

On the Thursday, Friday and Saturday of the third week in August, air raid sirens in the city were tested.

On 24 August the Bank of England doubled the bank rate, from two to four per cent.

Later in the month, residents in the area bounded by Constitution Hill and Mousehold Lane were asked to attend George White School to collect their gas masks. Respirators were not yet available for infants; instructions for these were to be given in the near future, but in the meantime distribution of adult masks continued.

There were appeals to the people of Norwich when thousands of children were evacuated from London to the Eastern Counties.

September

On the first of the month, five trainloads of evacuees arrived; five more would arrive on Saturday and seven more on Monday, each train bringing 1,000 people.

Norwich citizens were asked to help in the work of distribution by not congregating in the vicinity of Thorpe Station. The Town Clerk, Mr B.

D. Storey, said Norwich was still neither receiving nor evacuating at this time. Other than the fact that 16,000 children were expected to arrive at Thorpe Station over the next few days, Norwich had no part to play.

Work was hurriedly begun on air raid shelters for 35,000 people on the Norwich Cattle Market.

The Lord Mayor appealed for 100 ex-servicemen to volunteer for a National Defence Company for immediate duty in the city.

The use of factory sirens and hooters was prohibited except for giving air raid warnings.

A frightening letter appeared in the *Eastern Evening News* on 1 September. Signed by the Secretary of the RSPCA, it said: 'May I appeal through your columns to butchers in the towns and villages of Norfolk who possess humane killers, to offer their services to the local police for the purpose of destroying animals which have been hopelessly injured in air raids.'

In an atmosphere of increasing apprehension, people filled sand bags, bought black curtaining, dug Anderson shelters into their back gardens, collected small stocks of tinned foods – then looked at their children and at the small cardboard boxes that contained the gasmasks, smelling of pungent new rubber.

On the morning of 3 September the streets were strangely empty; fear of the unknown filled the air as people turned on their wireless sets to await the Prime Minister, Mr Neville Chamberlain. His words were heard with disbelief: 'This morning the British Ambassador in Berlin handed the German Government a final note stating that unless we heard from them by 11 o'clock that they were prepared at once to withdraw their troops from Poland, a state of war would exist between us. I have to tell you now that no such undertaking has been received and that consequently this country is at war with Germany.'

With stunned foreboding, the people realised that Norwich was at war.

Index

Adam and Eve Yard 24
aerodrome 25, 42
    see also airport
Agricultural Hall 11, 18, 25, 28, 75
air raid precautions 72, 77, 78, 82, 84, 85, 86,
        87–8
air raid shelters 87–8
air transport 70
aircraft 38, 40, 45
airport 51, 54, 56, 63
airships 13, 44, 47, 49
alastrim 57
Alderman Jex Senior Boys' School 86
Alexandra (pub) 66
Alexandra, Queen 34
aliens 47
Angel Road 17
Angel Yard 31
Appleyard, William 33
Arabian Horse Yard 31
Arcade 76
armistice 8
Assembly House 28, 64

Atkinson, Robert 51
Augustine Steward House 27, 32
autogiro 43

Backs (wine merchants) 26
Bailey, F. E. 46
Bailey, Peggy 79
Baker's Yard 34
Baldwin's Yard 31
Ball, H. W. 82
Bally Holdinstein 86
bands 64, 68, 78, 79
Bank Holidays 87
Bank Rate 47, 54, 87
Barclays Bank 38
Barfield and Richardson 56
Barker and Ramsbottom 64
Barnard, G. V. 76
Barnards Ltd 59
Barrack Street 65, 69
Bath House Yard 31
Bee Hive Yard 24
Bethel Street 69
    picture 50

Better Ole Club 31
betting 28
Bevan, Robert 36
Bevin, Ernest 76
billiards 50
Bircham Newton 40
Birkbeck, Geoffrey 83
Blakeney 21
Bloomfield, Mr (jeweller) 57
Bluebell 66
Blyth Secondary School 47
Boardman, Edward Thomas 32
Boar's Head, picture 76
boat race 58
Bolingbroke, Leonard 25, 33
Bolton, George 22
Bonds shop 37
boot and shoe manufacture 18, 49, 53–4, 61–3
    wages 12, 22
Bostock and Fitt 53
Boston's shop 61
Boulton & Paul 24, 38, 44, 47, 49, 70
Boundary Park Stadium 58, 59
bowls 52, 63

Bowthorpe 31–2
boxing 50, 65, 72, 77, 80
Brenner's Bazaar, picture 74
Bretts shop 53
Brickmakers pub 54
Briden, Harry 67
Bridewell 32, 33
Brown, Ernest 86
Browne garden, picture 35
Buckenham, Maidie 37, 41
Buckingham, Agnes 31
Buck's Yard 31
Bull Close school 21
Bullard & Sons 64
Bullough, Mr 79
Bunting, J. Walter 37
Buntings Stores 37, 60, 67
bus services 36–7, 47, 56, 58, 70
bus terminal 53
Bush Builders Ltd 54

Café Royal 80
Canada 34
Capitol cinema 60
Carlton cinema 56, 60, 65, 75
    organ 65
Carrow Bridge 25
Carrow Road football stadium 70, 83
cars 49, 64, 86
Casson, Lewis 75
Castle
    bones excavated at 67–8
    floodlighting 55
    picture 16
Castle Gardens 33
Castle Meadow, pictures 23
Castle Museum 20, 33, 41, 44, 60, 76
Cathedral
    cloister restored 80

memorial bronze 37
peace celebrations 13
throne restored 30
war memorial chapel 57
Watch Night service 34
Cathedral Close
    Cavell funeral 13
    Wellington statue 75
Cator, John 29
cattle market 16, 35, 46, 57
    fair at 74
Catton Grove 64
Cavell, Edith 12–13
Central Hall 72, 78
Chamberlin, G. M. 8
Chamberlin's Meadow 34
Chamberlin's shop 14, 26–7, 37
    picture 27
Chapelfield
    Drill Hall 19
    Gardens 28, 50, 64, 65, 85, 86
Chaplin's outfitters 53
Charing Cross 30
Chequers Yard 58
Christian Science church 68
cigarettes 74
Cinema (Magdalen Street) 72
Cinema Palace 28
cinemas 10, 18, 21, 28, 37, 41, 56, 60, 65, 68,
    78, 80, 82
    see also films
City Hall
    aerial photograph 81
    bronze doors 79
    bronze lions 78
    building first proposed 12, 44–5
    building sanctioned 58
    construction 69, 70, 73, 75, 84
    finance for 59, 65

need for 66
opening 83
plans 51
City Road 65
Clark, Mrs 12
Clarke, W. H. H. 38
Coach Makers Arms 77
Cohen, Percy 50, 68
Coleman, Ronald 24
Collins, J. 74
Colman, Alan R. 75
Colman, Ethel 46
Colman, Ethel Mary 29
Colman, Maria 31
Colman, Misses 33
Colman, Russell J. 17, 58, 63, 69, 83
Colman, Thomas William 86
Colmans 36, 82
Constitution (pub) 64
Copeman, John, & Sons Ltd 87
Corn Hall 50, 72, 77
Coslany Street 58
Costessey Mill 28
Cotman House 80–81
Cotman, John Sell 80
County Council offices 33
courts and yards *see* yards
Cowgate 65
Cranbox Ltd 50
crime rates 50, 86
Crome, John 20
Crome mill 61
Cromer 87
Crooks Place 10
Crotch, Walter 19, 20
Crown Point (Whitlingham) 43, 58
Crown Yard 24
Curl's 14, 45
    picture 37

Dain, J. H. (Chief Constable) 8, 13, 22, 31, 47, 50, 64, 84
    portrait 54
Dampier, Claude 76
dancing 68, 72, 78
Davidson, Harold F. 57–9
Davis, George 80
Davis, Joe 50
Delves Motors 37
Delves, S. 37
Dial Yard 31, 58
Distillery Yard 31, 58
Dog Yard 31
Doll's House 23
Drill Hall 19
drunkenness 31, 44, 64
Duff, Granville 21
Duke Street 43
Duncan, Sydney 40
Dunham, L. E. 60
Dunlop Company 40
Dyer, Fred 65

Eade, Peter 45
Earlham Estate 30, 78
Earlham Road 41, 62
earthquake 55
Eastern Daily Press 8, 39
Eastern Evening News 56
Eaton Golf Club 20, 21
Eaton Park 13, 29, 41–2
Edward and Edward 59
Edward VIII (King) 74
Eight Ringers Yard 31
Eisteddfod 40
elections 10, 22, 26, 29, 55, 84
Electric Cinema 10, 72, 75
Electric Theatre 13, 28
electricity supply 10, 12, 43, 79, 82

Elizabeth (Queen)
    at Cathedral 80
    at City Hall 83
    coronation 75
    as Duchess of York 29, 33
    husband becomes George VI 74
Elm Hill 29
Elmo Stores 86
Empire cinema 72
Empire Theatre 28
Enterprise cinema 68, 72
entertainment 24
    see also films; theatre; wireless
Exchange Street 50

Fairfax, J. Griffyth 29, 55
fairs 17, 74
farm workers' wages 21
Farrow Road 41
Farrow, Thomas 19, 20
Farrows Bank 19, 20
fascism 34, 63
Fasola, Cristofero 80
Fellmongers Yard 31
Fellows, William 41
Ferry House 78
Field, Sid 53
Fields, Gracie 73
films 22, 30, 45, 47, 51, 53, 56, 60, 65, 68, 72, 73, 75
    censorship 13
    see also cinemas
fire brigades 13, 45, 56, 82
fires 28, 43, 56, 61, 64, 67
Fish, H. 73
Fishmongers Arms 40–41
floods 21, 41
Flower Pot Yard 31
food rationing 9, 10

foot and mouth disease 17, 34, 77, 78
football 22, 34, 37, 46
    see also Norwich City Football Club
Formby, George, senior 53
Forster, Jack 50, 65
Fountain Yard 24
Fox, F. C. 67
Fox, Roy 79
Frankon, Ronald 24
Frazer, Herbert 74
Free Trade Tavern 66

Garlands 51, 61
gas masks 82
gas supply 12, 20
Gates, Charles 25
Gates, Eddie 65
George, David Lloyd 26
George V (King)
    death 71, 72
    inspects unemployment schemes 19–20
George VI (King)
    accession 74
    coronation 75
    as Duke of York 29, 33
    opens City Hall 83
    as Prince of Wales 41–3, 51, 52, 57, 63
Gill & Son 70
Globe Inn 65
Gloucester, Duke of 43
Goat Yard 31
Godfrey's 51
gold 57
Gorleston 52
Gowen, Herbert 35
Gray, Kenny 74
Gray, Olley 74
Green, Hughie 73, 77
Greenland Fishery Yard 31

Green's shop 14, 19
Green's Yard 24
greyhound racing 58, 59
Guild of Norwich Players 14
Guildhall 77
Guildhall Hill 14
    picture 8, 66
Gunton Sons & Dyball 43
Gurney, Eustace 26

Hall, H. E., & Co. 49
Hall, Henry 78
hangings 79
Hardiman, Alfred 78
Hardy, James 38
Hare, Doris 24
Harford Hall Estate 12, 46
Harmer, F. W. 43
Harmer's 28
Harrison, G. E., & Son Ltd 50
Harrison, V. E. 67
Hart, F. D. T. 19, 20
Hartland, Mr 55
Hawkes Yard 31
Hay, Will 53
Haymarket, pictures 35, 75
Haymarket Picture House 21, 22, 28, 45, 47,
        60, 72, 75, 82
    organ 55
    restaurant 26
Heigham Street 41
Henry, Leonard 24
Henry, Prince 31
Henson, Leslie 24
Hermitage 54
herrings 26, 52
Hindes, Mrs 12
Hippodrome 10, 26, 28, 53, 73, 76, 77, 78, 79
    picture 53

Hitler, Adolf 61
Holdinstein, Barry 86
Holloway, Stanley 24, 79
Holls Yard 31
Holmes, H. M. 33, 62
Holmes, Henry N. 38
horses 77–8
Horton's Yard 31
hospitals see isolation hospital; Jenny Lind
        Hospital; Lazar House; Norfolk and
        Norwich Hospital
housing 10, 12, 17, 19–20, 34, 40, 54, 64, 65,
        68, 70
Howes & Son Ltd 49
Howman's Yard 31

ice cream 26
Icehouse Lane 76
immigrants 47
influenza 9
International Stores 18
Ireland's cattle sale 57
isolation hospital 12
Ivory, Thomas 67

James, Charles Holloway 73
Jarrolds shop 22, 52, 55, 61, 74
Jarvis & Sons 24, 61, 79
Jay, Christopher 32
Jays shop 61
Jenny Lind Hospital 42, 72
Jewson, Dorothy 26, 27, 29, 55
Jewson, P. W. 70
Jex, F. C. 64, 67, 86
Johnson, Amy 54, 63
Johnson, G. F. 22–3
Jones, Frank 77

Kays Ways Pays shops 53

Key & Castle Yard 31
King Street 21

Lakenham 40
Lakenham School 14
Lambert, F. (tea merchant) 45
Lanchester, Elsie 75
Lauder, Harry 71, 76
Laurence Scott Electro Motors Ltd 67, 82, 86
Lawlor, Seaman Jim 72
Lazar House 26
Lee, Joseph 79
libraries 26, 76
licences 14, 24, 28, 60, 66
Lido 67, 68
Light Aeroplane Club of Norwich 40
Lincoln, Abraham 38
Lipton's 23
litter 49
Little Arabian Horse Yard 31
Little Brew Yard 31
Little Buck Yard 31
Little Queen Caroline Yard 31
Little, Walter (shop) 79
Littler, Prince 86
Lloyd, Marie 53
Lloyds Bank 38, 41, 76
London Street 8
Long, Norman 24, 79
Loose's 49
    picture 48
Lowestoft 21, 87
Low's House 69
lumber market, pictures 5

Mace's shop 61
Maddermarket 72
Magdalen Street 51
    picture 48

magistrates' court 8
Mann Egerton 25, 27, 79, 86
manufacturing 43
    see also boot and shoe manufacture;
        Boulton & Paul; Laurence Scott
        Electro Motors Ltd
Marchesi, Louis 24
Market Place
    accession celebrations 74
    armistice celebrations 8
    Fascist meeting 34
    May Day celebrations 35, 63
    new Provision Market 84
    stalls 72, 86
    Wellington statue 75
    pictures 2, 8, 9, 84
        aerial photo 81
Martham 17
Mary, Queen 59, 68
Masonic building 42
May Day 35, 63
Merton Road 72
Meyrick, F. J. 9
Middle Classes Union 20
Mile Cross Estate 19–20, 30
Mile Cross Road 25
Mitre pub 62
Mollison, Jim and Amy 63
Monck, Nugent 14, 36, 72
Moon's shop 61
Moore's shop 37, 85
Moray-Smith, J. 77
Morse, George Henry 23
Mosley, Sir Oswald 71
motor cars 49, 64, 86
motor cycles 10, 78
motor traffic 13, 40
    speed limit 66
Mountergate 24

Mousehold
    aerodrome 25, 43, 45, 51, 57
        picture 38
    heath 40, 64
    mill 61
    war memorial housing 42
municipal airport 56, 63
municipal offices 44–5
    demolition 80–81
    pictures 2, 6
Munnings, A. J. 44, 60
museums *see* Bridewell; Castle Museum;
        Strangers' Hall
Mustard Club 36
Mutual Service Club 75

National Kitchens 10
Natural Rose Day 72
Nest, The 22, 46, 49, 63, 64, 69, 71, 76
New Mills Yard 31
Nichols, Catherine Maude 23–4
Nickalls shop 10
Norfolk News Co. Ltd 8
Norfolk and Norwich Archaeological Trust 32
Norfolk and Norwich Art Circle 60, 83
Norfolk and Norwich Hospital 9, 38, 40, 41, 72
    carnival 55
    Colman memorial 83
    Nurses' Home opened 59
Norfolk and Norwich Savings Bank 45
Norfolk Pilgrim Society 38
North Earlham Estate 78
Norwich, street plan 7
Norwich Aero Club 38, 45, 66
Norwich Amateur Rowing Association 78
Norwich City Football Club 34, 37, 46, 49, 63,
        64, 69, 78, 83
    transfer fees 87
    see also Carrow Road; Nest

Norwich Girls High School 31, 64
Norwich Labour Club 64
Norwich Lads Club 31, 83–4
Norwich Mercury 22
Norwich Philharmonic Society 84
Norwich Players 14, 72
Norwich Swan Swimming Club 63
Norwich terriers 57
Norwich Unemployed Welfare Association 75
Norwich Union 38
Norwich Wireless Company 74
nursery schools 78

Oak Shades 66
Oak Street 30, 41, 58, 69
O'Brian, Bill 50
Odeon cinema 78
Old Brew Yard 31
    picture 9
Old Music House 14
Old Palace Road 41
Old Spring Gardens 24, 50, 52
Opera House 53
Orford Place, picture 37
organs
    Carlton cinema 65
    Haymarket cinema 55
Osborne's Yard 31
Oval (pub) 73

Page Bros 44
pageants 36
    aerial 40
pantomime 53, 72, 78
Park House (pub) 64
Parkinson, Sir Lindsay, & Co Ltd 70
parks 64
    see also Eaton Park; Waterloo Park;
        Wensum Park

Peacock's Bazaar, picture 74
Pembroke House School 18
photographs and the telegraph 50
Picture House (Haymarket) 21
Pierce, Stephen Rowland 73
Pilot Radio Services 74
Pipe Burners Yard 24, 65
Plough Yard 24
Pointer, Harry 70
police
    and armistice celebrations 8, 9
    and civil unrest 81
    and film censorship 13–14
    numbers 22, 54, 68
    offices 45, 66, 70
        picture 14
    pay 12, 14
    and public order 10–11, 34
    river patrols 54
    telephone system 50
poor law 34
poor rate 19
Pope, G. Stevens 33
Pottergate 45
power station 42, 43, 79
Prince of Wales Road 11
prison 14, 30, 79
pubs 31
    licensing hours 60

Queen Caroline pub 31
Queen Caroline Yard 31
Queen of Hungary Yard 24
Queen Victoria pub 31

radio 25, 27, 31, 56, 60, 74, 88
Ragged School Yard 31
railways
    Christmas services 34, 53

companies 23
    excursions 22, 43, 52, 56, 64, 87
    strike 27
Rampant Horse Street 10, 13, 14
    picture 67
Rank & Son Ltd 60
Rate Payers Association 20
rates 19, 23, 34, 85
rationing 9, 10
rats 12, 14–15
Rayne, Stanley Erico 80
Read, R. J. 57
records 60, 71
Red Flag 32, 34, 55
Red Rose (pub) 66
Reeve's Yard 24
refugees 85
Regal cinema 80
regatta 17, 63
Regent cinema 72, 75
Regent Theatre 28, 57
Remembrance Day 49
Rice, A. A. 42
Ridley's of Ipswich 47
Riley, Mr 78
Riley, Walter A. 73
Ritz cinema 82
river transport 70
Riverside Road 65
road surfaces 78–9
road traffic accidents 40
Roberts, G. H. 10, 12, 22–3
Robertson Colman Ltd 86
Robertson, Henry 86
Robey, George 76
Robinson Yard 30
Robinson's Yard 31
roller-skating 72, 78
Rose Day 25, 72

Rotary Club 33, 64
rowing 57, 78
Royal Arcade 76
Royal Hotel 71
Royal Norfolk Show 25, 43, 58
Royal Oak Yard 31
Rudd's Yard 31

Sadd, Ginger 65, 72, 77, 80
Sadler's Yard 31
St Andrew's Hall 42, 67, 75, 84
St Anne's church (Earlham) 59
St Benedict's 24
St Catherine's church (Mile Cross) 68
St Catherine's Plain 60
St Clement's Hill 40
St Giles 69
St Martin at Palace Plain 82
St Peter Mancroft church
    peace thanksgiving 8–9
    pictures 9, 69
St Peter's Street 45
St Stephen's gates 77
St Stephen's Street 40, 55
Samson and Hercules House 27, 32, 33, 78
Samuel, H. (jeweller) 45
Sandringham 72, 74
Saw Mill Yard 31, 58
Sayers, Dorothy L. 36
scarlet fever 85
School of Art 85
schools 40, 47, 67, 78, 86
    private 18, 31, 64
Scott, W. H. 82
Scott, Walter 17
Scottish fishing girls 52
Seaman, Kathleen 79
sewage works 78
Shakespeare, G. H. 55

Shamvas, Peggy 67, 79
Shapley, Brigadier General 8
sheep 16
Sheridan, Dinah 75
shoes
    fashions 49, 61
    see also boot and shoe manufacture
Shopping Week 51
Silver Jubilee celebrations (1936) 68, 69
smallpox 41, 45, 47, 57
Smith, C. Herbert 46
Smith, R. W. 26, 29
Smith, W. R. 55
Smith, Walter 79
Smith's Yard 31
South Park Avenue 42
Southill, James, and Company 12
speed limit 66
speedway 80
    stadium 57
Spelman's sale yard 57
sports stadium (Hellesdon) 58
Spring Gardens 24, 50, 52, 60
    ballroom 64
    Pavilion 24
    Theatre 51
Steward and Patteson Ltd 54, 64, 80
Stiffkey, Rector of 57–9
Storey, Bernard D. 84, 87
Strangers' Hall 25, 30, 33
strikes 22, 27, 28, 35, 75, 76
Suckling House 32, 33, 46
Suffolk Arms Yard 31
Sun Yard 31
Sunday opening 41
Swan Yard 31
swimming 63

Talbot Yard 31

taxis 2, 14
Taylor, W. J. F. 70
teachers' salaries 16
Technical College 85
telegraph 50
telephone exchanges 52, 78
telephones, and police 50
television broadcasts 73
Temple, Shirley 82
Territorial Army 86
Thatched Restaurant 57, 68
Thatched Theatre 28, 30
theatre 14
Theatre de Luxe 18, 28, 72
Theatre Royal 35, 36, 53, 63, 71, 72, 73, 75,
    76, 78, 86, 87
    fire 67
    rebuilt 70
theatres 28, 53
Thorn, Beatrice 31
Thorndyke, Sybil 75
Thorpe Hamlet Senior Girls' School 67
Thorpe station 53
Three Kings Yard 24
Thurston, Charles
    early film shows 65
    fair 17
Thurston family 74
tobacco 10, 74
Tombland, *see also* Augustine Steward House;
    Samson and Hercules House
Tombland Fair 17, 74
Trades Union Congress 76
traffic lights 47
Trafford, S. W. 40
trams 22, 27–8, 36–7, 58, 61, 64, 71
    last lines removed 79
    pictures 15, 37, 66
Trim, Mrs 12

True Comrade (pub) 66
tuberculosis 12
Tuns Yard 31
Turners Court 24

unemployment 18, 34, 43, 55, 60, 66, 84–5
    benefit 12, 17, 19, 34, 86
    work schemes 25, 29, 34, 41, 50, 62
Unicorn Yard 31
United Bus Company 47
university 12, 18
Unthank Road 10, 18

Valori, G. 26
vandalism 54
Venetian Ballroom 68

Waggon and Horse Yard 58
Walk, The 38, 41, 45
    armistice celebrations 8
    at election time 55
    pictures 15
Walker, W. E. 42
Wallace King shops 53
Wallace, Nellie 63, 77, 87
war memorial 40, 42, 83
Warminger, Alfred 65, 68
Watch Committee 13
water supply 19
Waterloo Park 62, 64, 75
Watling, Charles F. 70, 71, 77, 78, 79, 83
Wayne, Nauton 24
weather 47, 61, 64, 71, 72, 76, 85
weather forecasts 49
wedding photograph 4
Wells-next-the-sea 21
Wensum Park 29
Wensum View School 47
Westlegate 73

Westwick Depot 77
White Lion Yard 31
Whitefriars Bridge 29
Whitlingham 17
Whitlingham Gardens 63
Whitlingham Reach 63
Wild Man (pub) 66
Willmotts shop 60, 71, 79
wireless 25, 27, 31, 56, 60, 74, 88
Witard, Herbert E. 10, 22–3, 40, 42, 51
    portrait 40

Wolferton 72
women 46
Wood Entry Yard 65
Woodbastwick Hall 29
Woodford, James 79
Woolworth's 46, 54
workhouse 31–2
Wounded Hart Lane 69
Wroxham Estate 40

yacht station 65, 70

yards 24–5, 30
Yare River 21, 63
Yare Rowing Club 57
Yarmouth 21, 52, 87
Yaxleys shop 59
York, Duke and Duchess of 29, 33
Young, Edward Hilton 10, 22–3, 29
Young Women's Christian Association 32, 33
Youngs Crawshay & Youngs 73